The Psycho˙

"As a psychologist and former presiden⌐
chology, I have seen Brexit concerns in ⌐   ...st hand.
But depth of psychological analysis has ⌐   ⌐.. ⌐n short supply. Brian
Hughes fills this gap with a penetrating analysis of the impact on citizens and
communities, written with energy and style. One that I think will earn an
enduring place on the Brexit bookshelf."
—Nicola Gale, Department of Psychology, City, University of London
and Former President of the British Psychological Society

"This book is an articulate and insightful enquiry into the psychology of
Brexit. Brian Hughes draws upon theories from cognitive psychology, social
psychology and individual differences to explain what compelled a majority of British people who turned out at the ballot box to vote to leave the
European Union, and the psychological consequences of this collective decision. Hughes's accessible and absorbing style makes this a must-read for anyone interested in human behaviour and decision-making."
—Michael Smith, Associate Professor of Psychology, Northumbria
University, UK

"This book is a must-read for politicians, academics, and teachers, as well as
the layperson. In this excellent and clearly written volume, Hughes has illus-
trated the integral connection between political decisions and psychological
well-being and as such this book is in the vanguard of the area. Politicians need
to be cognizant that their decisions impact not only the political and economic
future of their countries, but also they can seriously impact the mental health
of their citizens."
—Esther Greenglass, Professor of Psychology, York University, Toronto, Canada

"Political circumstances are inherent companions of human experience, bringing gains and losses, rewards and costs, regardless of whether or not they are directly or indirectly influenced and/or experienced. It's no surprise then, particularly to social scientists, to discover how much politics affect our psychological beings. Yet the psychological dynamics that govern political processes and outcomes may be less obvious, particularly to politicians. Hughes's timely, insightful and brave analysis of the psychology of politics of Brexit is a lesson for all."

—Krys Kaniasty, *Distinguished Professor of Psychology, Indiana University of Pennsylvania, USA, and Institute of Psychology, Polish Academy of Sciences, Poland*

Brian M. Hughes

The Psychology of Brexit

From Psychodrama to Behavioural Science

Brian M. Hughes
School of Psychology
National University of Ireland, Galway
Galway, Ireland

ISBN 978-3-030-29363-5   ISBN 978-3-030-29364-2   (eBook)
https://doi.org/10.1007/978-3-030-29364-2

Cover credit: mspoint/shutterstock.com

This Palgrave Macmillan imprint is published by the registered company Springer Nature Switzerland AG
The registered company address is: Gewerbestrasse 11, 6330 Cham, Switzerland

To my parents,
Mary and Jarlath

Acknowledgements

I would like to thank everyone at Palgrave for their work on this book, with particular thanks to Beth Farrow for her support and guidance. I am also grateful to Jo O'Neill.

I am extremely thankful to a number of colleagues and contacts who have provided their advice and feedback. I am fortunate to have been able to call on specialists in many different areas (nonetheless, all errors of fact or judgement are of course my own). Special thanks to Aidan Kane, Donncha O'Connell, Marie-Louise Coolahan, Marguerite Hughes, and Siobhán Howard for reading drafts of various sections, and for their expert feedback. I am also grateful to a number of others for sharing their ideas, thoughts, and Brexit perspectives, including Krys Kaniasty, Páraic Ó Súilleabháin, Chris Snowdon, Esther Greenglass, and John Bogue. Some of the thoughts on these pages I rehearsed at a public lecture for the Psychological Society of Ireland, and I am thankful to all at PSI for arranging this, including Terri Morrissey and Lisa Stafford.

As always, I want to pay personal tribute to the usual gang for their constant support and patience, to Annie and Louis, and, especially, Marguerite.

Brian M. Hughes

Also by Brian M. Hughes

Conceptual and Historical Issues in Psychology (2012, Prentice-Hall)
Rethinking Psychology: Good Science, Bad Science, Pseudoscience (2016, Palgrave)
Psychology in Crisis (2018, Palgrave)

Contents

1

Brexit as Psychodrama

'THE EMPIRE STRIKES BACK' shouted the headline, its huge white letters consuming almost the entire front page. It was one of those days when the news needed to be announced in block capitals. In the background was a barely visible greyed-out Union Flag, worn away, no doubt, by winds of destruction, while below, a cut-out of Prime Minister David Cameron gazed offstage, his pained face signalling defeat to the world.

With clichéd but nonetheless vivid visual cues, this tabloid headline proclaimed a unique historical juncture, a moment in time that few readers would ever truly forget (Miranda, 2016).

It was the day after the Brexit referendum. Against every expectation, the people had voted *Leave*. 'Get us out of here,' they said. Britain, and perhaps the world, would never be the same again.

But while it was certainly eye-catching and suitably dramatic, the headline was a little curious just the same. Something did not quite add up.

Precisely what 'EMPIRE' was being referred to?

Was this an allusion to the United Kingdom's self-styled standing as an imperial power, whose global relevance owes more to historical and cultural nostalgia than to actual territorial dominion?

© The Author(s) 2019
B. M. Hughes, *The Psychology of Brexit*,
https://doi.org/10.1007/978-3-030-29364-2_1

Or was it a reference to the European Union itself, a pan-national expansionist consortium, often accused by Eurosceptics of having imperialist intentions of its own?

As with all things Brexit, matters were more complicated than they first appeared. As we will see throughout this book, quite what everything means depends largely on your perspective.

At least the notion of 'empires' 'striking' at each other was appropriately apocalyptic. It was beginning to feel as though reality was falling apart. Within hours of the referendum result, the Prime Minister had announced his resignation. The value of the pound—and of the euro—plummeted on global currency markets. The world's media began to obsess about the implications of this unexpected sociopolitical meltdown.

And in the United Kingdom, Brexit was quickly becoming an all-consuming, collectively traumatising, and supremely challenging social upheaval.

For want of a better term, in the years since 2016, Brexit has unfolded into a fully-fledged psychodrama.

In the media, academia, and the public square, there is an ever-present impulse to explain Brexit in psychological terms, albeit with varying degrees of convincingness. Brexit attitudes are frequently projected as symptoms of pathological thought. People who voted Remain are labelled 'Remoaners', implying the presence of chronically disordered mood. Those who voted Leave are dismissed as 'Brextremists', which hints at sociopathy.

The language of psychiatry is often used to decry Brexit as an act of national 'self-harm', with little apparent regard for the sensitivities of people for whom *actual* self-harm is a lived reality. This so-called national self-harm of Brexit is sometimes depicted as a catastrophe; at other times, it is employed to titillate readers by implying a nationwide predilection for masochism.

Other perspectives focus on political performance. They analyse the group dynamics and organisational behaviours required to achieve the best bureaucratic Brexit. The entire enterprise, ostensibly the crafting of a new national sovereignty on an unprecedentedly grand scale, is reduced to the grubby realities of personality clashes and the needs of internal party management.

For many people, the psychological impact of Brexit is the challenge of its complexity. Brexit melts the brain. Its incomprehensibility is a source of national distress. In a daytime chat show interview that went viral on social media, the actor Danny Dyer spoke for millions when he declared Brexit to be 'a mad riddle' about which 'no-one's got a f***ing clue' (Busby, 2018).

Brexit is not the result of accidental tragedy or spontaneous economic turmoil. It was contrived by politicians, was voted for by citizens, and is now being implemented by bureaucrats.

Brexit did not 'just happen.' It exists because people decided to make it exist. It is therefore hugely influenced by a myriad of psychological factors as experienced across many social groups. Brexit is the combined reflection of a multitude of perceptions, preferences, choices, self-images, attitudes, ideas, assumptions, and reasoned (or ill-reasoned) conclusions.

So if you want to understand Brexit, why not turn to a psychologist?

After all, psychology is the formal study of these very human behaviours, these emotions and thoughts, these experiences of individuals and communities. Psychology is a science (more or less) in that it seeks empirical evidence to support or reject given claims.

Psychologists develop theories, conduct experiments, and gather data. They look for signals in what would otherwise be treated as noise. They seek to impose intellectual order on worldly chaos.

And what could be more chaotic than Brexit?

The Psychologising of Brexit

Brexit is unavoidably relevant, and not just to British audiences. It is a case study in group decision-making within mass democratic systems; its lessons speak to any community where choices are made at ballot boxes. It took one of the most advanced societies ever to have existed and turned it into a place of prevalent and near-permanent pandemonium. It is a warning to all other peaceable countries against cultural complacency.

And in disrupting the balance of society—in wrecking its resting homeostasis—Brexit is the very definition of what psychologists refer to as a 'stressor.' It can therefore be presumed to be inflicting a grievous mental load on the population.

Brexit emerged from psychological impulses, was determined by psychological choices, is construed in terms of psychological perceptions, and will leave a lasting psychological imprint. For many people, especially in the United Kingdom (but not only there), Brexit looms large in the psyche. It should be no surprise then, when pundits try to explain it, that Brexit's psychological dimensions receive so much airtime.

But not all hot takes are equal. Sometimes the interpretation of events reveals more about the people doing the interpreting than it does about the events themselves. The very idea that Brexit reflects a British yearning for past imperial glories may well be a case in point. This is important because such imperialist narratives have been used not only to explain Brexit, but also to demonise those who support it.

The notion that centuries of history intrude upon the behaviour of citizens alive today offers a highly seductive narrative. However, with any psychological approach, it is important to consider empirical evidence and scientific standards of reasoning. This is because seductive narratives are themselves propelled by psychological influences. In many cases, they are often seductive precisely because they are divorced from real-world banality.

In other words, many seductive narratives are examples of escapism.

They are seductive precisely because they are wrong.

Empire 2.0

It is in the psychological nature of humans to consider one's own kind exceptional. In this regard, the humans who make up the modern United Kingdom are, well, no exception.

Britons are generally aware that the United Kingdom has had a significant impact on the world. Few nations can claim to have impacted the world more. At one time or another, the British have forcibly invaded all but twenty-two of the countries that make up the current international community (Laycock, 2012).

It seems that Britain has been looking to take things over for as long as history has been written: one of the first recorded mentions of the British was when Julius Caesar wrote about them turning up, unexpectedly, fighting the Romans in France.

The first formal British endeavour to topple another state—an invasion of Gaul led by Clodius Albinus in AD 197—got no further than Lyon. However, over successive centuries, Britain went on to accumulate a slew of dominions, colonies, territories, and protectorates. Britain ruled the waves 'at heaven's command' and built a commonwealth that spanned the globe. Its truly global reach prompted George Macartney, the Irish-born governor of the British West Indies, to declare it a 'vast empire on which the sun never sets, and whose bounds nature has not yet ascertained' (Kenny, 2006).

In the United Kingdom, schoolchildren are taught that, at its peak, the British Empire comprised a quarter of the earth's land area as well as a quarter of its population. The concept is ingrained in citizens' minds from an early age. Whether all its ramifications are appreciated is less clear.

Occasionally, the statistic is garbled, as when a caller to national radio claimed that citizens should have no fears about a post-Brexit future, because their country used to control 'three thirds of the world.' When challenged, the caller reduced this to 'two thirds' (Oppenheim, 2017). Past glories are often more influential in essence than in substance.

Public commentary and media coverage regularly locates Brexit within a post-imperial frame. For academic Nadine El-Enany (2017), the Brexit vote reflected a long-held anxiety about loss of empire. This created for Britain an 'extreme discomfort at its place as, formally, an equal alongside other EU member states', rather than holder of the imperial throne. Vince Cable, leader of the Liberal Democrats, argued that many Brexit supporters are addled by 'nostalgia for a world where passports were blue, faces were white, and the map was coloured imperial pink' (Jamieson, 2018).

Academics and journalists have described how a 'nostalgic yearning for lost colonies' has become deeply embedded as 'part of [Britain's] national psyche' (Olusoga, 2017). It creates a condition of 'postcolonial melancholia' that continues to distort political debate (Saunders, 2019). Britain suffers a recurring 'self-deluded narrative' about its prospects for new imperial exploits, where '"our" former colonies will want to form a new, white,

English-speaking trading area—nicknamed Empire 2.0—to replace the EU' (Mason, 2018).

A theme of pathological self-aggrandisement appears repeatedly. According to *Guardian* writer Gary Younge (2018):

> Our colonial past, and the inability to come to terms with its demise, gave many the impression that we are far bigger, stronger and more influential than we really are. At some point they convinced themselves that the reason we are at the centre of most world maps is because the Earth revolves around us, not because it was us who drew the maps.

In their book, *Rule Britannia: Brexit and the End of Empire*, geographer Danny Dorling and sociologist Sally Tomlinson warn that such post-imperial 'arrogance' fuels Brexit, because 'a small number of people in Britain have a dangerous, imperialist misconception of our standing in the world' (Dorling & Tomlinson, 2019).

The post-imperial slant is not confined to British commentary. It has been adopted around the world as journalistic shorthand for reporting on Brexit. The *New York Times* records Brexit as 'England's last gasp of Empire', a 'misguided craving' that plays on a 'fantasy of revived greatness' promoted by 'dreamers' who are 'sickened by nostalgia' (Judah, 2016). In the *Washington Post*, Britain's 'old colonial hubris' is depicted as causing the United Kingdom to 'cling to imperial nostalgia,' weighed down by 'a fair amount of delusion' (Tharoor, 2019).

In *Le Monde*, French historian Jean-François Dunyach complains of how British Eurosceptics deploy empire myths as 'ideological accessories,' comprised of little more than 'irreducible ambiguities' (Dunyach, 2019). American historian Dane Kennedy depicts Brexit as being permanently propelled by 'repeated evocations of the imperial past' (Kennedy, 2018).

All this talk combines to produce an elaborate psychological model—a theory if you will—that posits a clear role for deep-rooted empire-thinking in shaping today's events. As Dorling and Tomlinson put it, Brexit represents 'the last vestiges of empire working their way out of the British psyche.'

At first glance, it seems to add up. The very fact that Britain ruled the waves before would appear to provide *prima facie* evidence that it is capable of doing so again. This makes British prosperity a tangible possibility in people's minds, and not merely a hypothesis.

But there is more to this psychodrama than a past that role-models the future. It is not just a case of learning logical lessons that allow you to imitate history. In this analysis, there are mysterious forces such as 'delusion', 'melancholia', 'yearning', 'discomfort', and 'nostalgia' and, of course, the amorphous 'British psyche.' With visceral drivers of thoughts, emotions, and behaviour operating on a collective national mind, this is a theory of Brexit that describes a people simultaneously overwhelmed by distorting impulsivity and incapable of true logic.

The effects of this type of thing should be wide-ranging. To assert that British people really are weighed down by colonial anxieties, imperial hang-ups, and delusions of majesty is to describe a kind of brain-addling sickness that subverts the very process of democracy. It is to imply that the British, or at least some of them, are *not of sound mind.* Such a claim should place the psychology of Brexit at the very centre of daily life.

From Self-Regard to Self-Loathing

But before we address its merits, let's take a moment to see where else this line of *Brexit-as-post-imperial-psychodrama* might take us. One consequence of no longer leading an empire is that the British people must now explain—to themselves, mainly—why it is their status is so reduced. Decades of psychological research show how most people are unlikely to account for losses by simply taking the blame themselves. Instead, they engage in various kinds of rationalisation process, where personal histories get re-written after the fact.

One approach involves finding a scapegoat, someone to blame for one's plight. Often scapegoats are accused of precisely those failings that the accusers themselves feel guilty of. In other words, people end up 'projecting' their own failings onto others. In couples therapy, a self-centred client might attempt to shift unwanted criticism by arguing that their *partner* is the one who is really greedy. Such rationalisations might succeed in deflecting blame in the here and now, but they are unlikely to produce long-lasting happiness.

A second strategy is to try to transfigure discomfort into something that feels more positive. For example, a client who feels their partner is selfish could decide that they actually *love* the fact that their partner is, in fact, so 'self-assured'. Reframed in such terms, the client's uncomfortable situation becomes a source of positive emotions, rather than negative ones, albeit superficially and precariously so.

When adopted knowingly, these rationalisations can be seen as useful coping strategies, excuses that can be rolled out when seeking to avoid guilt. However, when earnestly believed, such excuses become something else. They become pathological delusions, beliefs in falsehoods, psychotic thoughts, disconnections from reality. They become *symptoms*. This symptomatic scenario is inherent in the depiction of Brexit as a post-imperial psychodrama.

Some accounts of Brexit attempt to tease out these ancillary notions, looking for signs that confirm the merit of the overall interpretation. Thus, it is said, the British people are frequently driven to find consolation by casting 'faceless Brussels bureaucrats' as an 'out-group' on whom they can project their own record of poor judgement (Carswell, 2018).

For example, British critics have frequently decried the European Union for failing to restrict immigration to the United Kingdom. However, for years, the UK authorities have had the power to regulate this for themselves (Lee, 2018). In other words, British Eurosceptics—many of whom are parliamentarians—blame the EU for looking the other way on migration; when, in fact, it is the elected UK parliament—in other words, many of those self-same Eurosceptics—who are the real culprits.

From Self-Loathing to Self-Abuse

The scapegoating strategy is often supplemented by an effort to seek solace in suffering. One lesson from psychology research is that human beings find it quite easy to re-purpose their emotions in light of circumstance. In fact, they do it all the time, often without realising.

In a famous 1960s experiment, psychologists in the University of Minnesota injected students with adrenaline without telling them what was in the syringe (Schachter & Singer, 1962). They then convinced the students that their strange physical reactions were actually due to emotional responses rather than to drug effects. Importantly, the psychologists were able to *choose* what particular emotions the students ended up feeling. They convinced some of the students that their physical reactions were due to anger by saying annoying things to them. They convinced other students that their stimulation resulted from happiness by telling them jokes. All the students experienced the same physical adrenaline rush, but how it was interpreted depended entirely on what the psychologists *decided* they should feel. The study revealed how human beings are quite capable of re-interpreting their own emotions *after they begin to feel them.*

The implication is one of the most important principles of psychology: *human beings are greatly influenced by others—and are never as in control of their feelings and perceptions as they like to think they are.*

Because of this, people can even learn to *enjoy* wallowing in pain, or at least to feel affirmed by the experience. The identification with the role of 'pain-recipient' eventually drives them towards self-destructive behaviour. According to Irish journalist Fintan O'Toole, these very psychological ideas can be used to explain Brexit. O'Toole presents a particularly pulsating account of this view in his book *Heroic Failure: Brexit and the Politics of Pain* (O'Toole, 2018), where he claims to catalogue several vivid examples of a 'sadopopulist' dynamic in British culture.

For example, he draws parallels between the 1970s punk movement—with its message of 'masochism as revolt'—and the 'nihilistic energy that helped to drive the Brexit impulse.' 'Punk took bondage gear out of the bedroom and on to the street,' he argues, while 'Brexit took coterie self-pity out of the media-political boudoir and into real politics.'

O'Toole juxtaposes the popular sadomasochistic penchant for Nazi uniforms alongside the World War II jingoism so repeatedly invoked by pro-Leave campaigners. He points to the unique popularity in Britain of so-called 'alternative history' novels in which the United Kingdom is depicted as having lost the war, and been subjugated by Fascists. Could this be, O'Toole asks, a sign that British people hold a deep sense of being dominated by, say, the European Union?

He goes on to note how 'the biggest-selling book by an English author' in the years leading up to the Brexit referendum was E. L. James's *Fifty Shades of Grey*, an erotic romance novel heavily reliant on themes of dominance, submission, and sadomasochism (James, 2012). O'Toole suggests that the 'vicarious bondage' that readers enjoyed when reading the book revealed a receptiveness to the broader political narrative that pro-Brexit advocates would later put to them: namely, that the United Kingdom is itself in bondage to the European Union. Again, the idea here is that cultural tastes reveal the inner feelings of (many) British people, a deep-seated sense of victimhood reframed as a relish for masochism.

O'Toole is not the only commentator to imply that masochism is an energising force in the Brexit experience. Political discussion often centres on the idea. The claim that the pain of a hard Brexit is 'a price worth paying'—essentially, that suffering would be good for the country—is a recurring theme. In parliament, the House of Commons leader of the Scottish National Party explicitly decried such views as amounting to 'masochism', saying they involved 'delusion, deafness, self-flagellation—which [the Conservatives] have obviously found a taste for,' as well as 'schism, paralysis and then eventual political death' (O'Donoghue, 2019).

The argument that these forces serve only to perpetuate support for Brexit, rather than impede it, is confirmed by the results of several opinion polls. In such surveys, a majority of Leave voters usually say that Britain should withdraw from the European Union regardless of the economic damage it would cause, and even if it resulted one of their own family members becoming unemployed (Mance, 2017).

Therein lies the end-point of psychodrama. The British (or as O'Toole would emphasise, the English) have lost their once glorious empire and now drift on, forever psychically wounded. They learn to wallow in a xenophobic victimhood. They become obsessed with, but simultaneously demonise, their Brussels-based abusers. Ultimately, and inevitably, they bring about their own wilful, self-designed, and self-administered destruction. As psychological narratives go, it is all certainly very thorough.

However, simply juxtaposing two ideas never proves that one thing causes another. Psychology involves much more than the construction of a thorough narrative. Science requires that narratives be tested against rigorous decision-making logic and, where possible, objective empirical evidence. We can all recognise the psychodrama as exciting, colourful, and eye-catching. But that, unfortunately, doesn't make it real.

A Scientific Psychology of Brexit

Psychology can be a difficult science precisely because of how interesting it is. Its subject matter is the stuff of daily conversation. Few topics in, say, nuclear physics get discussed across the dinner table. However, the meat and drink of psychology is consumed at every meal. By default, all human conversation reduces to the stuff of psychology: Who did what? Why did they do it? And will they do it again? To paraphrase Homer, in some ways, we are *all* psychologists. However, to paraphrase Homer Simpson, in other—more *accurate*—ways, we are not.

Psychology is not punditry. In many senses, it is its opposite. While punditry affords the opportunity to put forward a subjective expert assessment, psychology—as a scientific field—seeks to *circumvent* the notion of subjective assessment. Instead, psychology constructs explanations by outsourcing the drawing of conclusions to a formal method.

The reasons for doing so have been illuminated by psychology itself. We have discussed some of them above. Specifically, when left to their own devices, human beings are much less objective than they think they are. Therefore, it behoves them to be vigilant to their own subjectivity, to resist their own biases, and to take deliberate steps to produce objective conclusions. This is why humanity invented the scientific method, and why psychology, unlike punditry, came to be a science.

That is not to say that all psychologists wear white coats, inhabit laboratories, crunch numbers, or are men (Hughes, 2016). Science is not a uniform, a place, or a ritual. Rather, science is what philosophers call a 'way of knowing,' an epistemology. It is an alternative to opinion, hearsay, instinct, authority, or superstition. It is true that most sciences focus on numerical data that have been gathered under controlled conditions, such as in laboratory experiments. However, scientific reasoning does not require these particular logistical features. Science requires things to be demonstrable, disprovable (potentially), and replicable. If these conditions can be met— in reality, or *merely in principle*—then one's reasoning can be said to be scientific.

It is possible to take a scientific approach to curing disease, tackling climate change, or designing automobiles. It is also possible to take a scientific approach to dealing with racism, raising children, or choosing where to go on holiday.

Of course, it is possible too to take a scientific approach to understanding the psychology of Brexit. We can consider the post-imperial psychodrama of Brexit to be our first example.

Psychodrama Under the Microscope

There is no doubt that cultural immersion is real and that, throughout their lives, people are bombarded with propaganda. However, those who voted in the Brexit referendum or who now steer its implementation have all lived finite lives in the modern era. Therefore, the first question we might ask is: is it really true that historic events, such as the demise of empire, offer important insights into the reasons so many people are animated by Brexit today?

At its most rudimentary, we can consider the post-imperial psychodrama theory in terms of its *cause-and-effect* structure. The 'demise of the British Empire' is the proposed cause, support for Brexit the proposed effect. Of course, this is all very simplistic. No analyst would claim that there is only one cause of Brexit. We would certainly consider Brexit to be a *multi-causal* affair. But that doesn't remove the core *cause-and-effect* relationship that is being proposed. To illustrate: even though the causes of heart disease are likely to be many, and are likely to compound each other's effects, it is still reasonable to ask whether red meat on its own is a risk factor we should worry about.

When we hear about a proposed cause-and-effect relationship, we often jump to the conclusion that the cause is the cause and the effect is the effect. In reality, without further evidence, the most we can say is that two events have occurred. Simply by happening in the same universe, the purported cause and effect are 'correlated'. But, as is reasonably well known, *correlation* and *causation* are not the same thing. Just because two things happen together doesn't mean that one caused the other. It could be that the other caused the one. It could be that some third thing caused them both. Or it could just all be a coincidence. In other words, there might be no relationship whatsoever between the two events.

Jumping to causality conclusions is very human. We all do it thousands of times a day. When you hear water droplets pinging on a window pane, and then see dark clouds in the sky behind, your brain immediately intuits that it is raining (in other words, that the clouds have 'caused' the droplets). You form this conclusion without having to dwell on the matter. It is a sign of the efficiency of your brain, the basic biology of which you share with all other humans, an organ that has evolved over the millennia to be good at detecting patterns.

Of course, the problem is that not all patterns are meaningful. Sometimes there will be another reason for those water droplets. But because our brains have evolved to be, effectively, pattern-detecting engines, we bias towards seeing causality whenever we spot a correlation. It is a powerful instinct that is very hard to resist.

For example, in January 2019 a group of MPs attempted to pass a motion in the House of Commons (the so-called 'Cooper amendment') that would extend the Brexit negotiating period beyond what was then the deadline of 29 March. However, the government, led by Prime Minister Theresa May, successfully defeated that motion, going on to pass a further measure of their own (the 'Brady amendment') that preserved their intended negotiating strategy. The next day, on currency markets, the pound fell in value by a cent against the US dollar (Elliott, 2019). Critics of the government declared this to be a cause-and-effect event, arguing that the markets were responding to the votes in parliament. Of course, this might have been true, in that currency investors would be wise to take political decisions into account when deciding whether or not to buy sterling. However, currencies usually decline in value when the government of the day suffers *defeat* in parliament, not when it wins its key votes. Therefore, while pundits might have declared the fall in the pound to be an obvious effect of parliamentary causes, they would have found it just as easy to interpret a *rise* in the pound in cause-and-effect terms as well.

In short, correlations offer seductive narratives whichever direction they point. *Either* falls *or* increases in the pound can be declared to be meaningful. But it can hardly be that two opposing scenarios reveal equally worthy insights. More likely, they don't reveal that many insights at all.

Our pattern-detecting brains extract too much signal from what is effectively noise.

If it is difficult to attribute causality between one day's parliamentary votes and the next day's currency fluctuations, you can imagine how hard it must be to draw causal links between the fall of the British Empire and twenty-first century Brexit.

When we jump to a causality conclusion and it turns out to be wrong, we call this a 'correlation fallacy'. It happens quite a lot. To avoid it, scientific reasoning usually tests a theory against a number of alternative explanations. Loosely speaking, a scientific assessment will ask whether a claimed causal effect could in fact be explained by chance, whether it is overly reliant on eye-catching information, whether it is contradicted by counterexamples, or whether any simpler theories could do the job better. Let us consider how the Brexit-as-post-imperial-psychodrama theory fares under such scrutiny.

The Problem of Improbability

Sometimes, after they happen, historical events begin to look almost like they were inevitable. We perceive them as reflecting a kind of historical 'logic', as though they reveal an inherent order in the passage of time. To some extent, this again reflects the way our brains are primed to detect patterns, even when patterns are not really there. We apply narratives to history in order to make sense of it. The alternative, the idea that history might simply be, to quote Alan Bennett, 'just one bloody thing after another,' strikes us as deeply unsatisfying.

This is accentuated by the way we summarise events in order to explain them, whether we are journalists, historians, or interested citizens. All summaries are, by definition, adulterated versions of real events. Pertinent details are usually emphasised, or 'sharpened.' Less pertinent ones are downplayed, or 'levelled.' These are natural processes of storytelling. We use them to ensure that our explanations of events stay relevant. Were we to bombard our audience with microscopic details or trivial descriptions, then the true point of our explanations might well be lost.

Sharpening and levelling are important features of how humans communicate, and greatly affect the way information spreads through social communication channels. The psychology of human interaction continues to play a huge part in shaping the events around Brexit today. We will look at this in detail in Chapter 3.

Our brains too engage in sharpening and levelling when we process memories into long-term storage. We often think of our memories as a kind of facsimile document, a video of events that we replay in our mind's eye whenever we want to recall something. However, in reality, most human memories—even the most personally important ones—are adulterated summary-depictions of what really happened. We write memories into our brains in a way that preserves and falsely accentuates the most important points.

As with many other situations, our pattern-detecting brains are often over-sensitive. They err towards false positives, seeing many sequences that simply do not exist. Rather than detecting patterns in the information that flows our direction, our brains seek to *impose* a pattern on everything, in order to make simplified sense of otherwise overwhelming complexity.

From the psychology of perception and reasoning, we know that our innate pattern-detection bias serves us well in most cases. However, in some situations, it causes significant problems. One of our biggest challenges is interpreting information that is just too complicated to absorb. We are especially poor at comprehending probability, chance, and randomness.

When we hear Brexit described as the consequence of post-imperial malaise, our immediate reaction is to see the sense in the narrative. However, we should bear in mind that our instinct is to downplay the complexity of events. We lose sight of the role of serendipity—of pot luck—in determining outcomes. When we take this idea of chance properly into account, the post-imperial psychodrama looks a lot less convincing.

For example, the very fact that there was even a Brexit referendum was itself largely a chance occurrence. Prime Minister David Cameron proposed the idea in a party conference speech in January 2013. However, at that time, most political experts agreed that Cameron would never be required to fulfil this undertaking. This was because it was assumed that the Conservative party could not win a majority in the subsequent election. Instead, they would have to form another coalition with the

Liberal Democrats, who would not permit a Brexit referendum to proceed. In committing to this future promise at no cost, Cameron was exercising a highly rational choice, given the normal human imperative to avoid unnecessary risk. He could appease those within his party who wanted a symbolic promise to be made, without ever having to actually follow through on making that promise reality.

Prior to the general election of 2015, opinion polls were as one in forecasting a hung parliament. Of the eleven polls published in the final week of the campaign, five of them predicted a dead heat, in which the Conservatives and Labour would each attract the same vote share. Averaging across the polls suggested the Conservatives would receive no more than 33.6% of votes. The BBC concluded that the Conservatives would fall short of a parliamentary majority by some fifty seats, opening the door to a possible coalition between Labour and the Scottish National Party. In reality, when the real voters cast their real votes in the real election, the Conservative party swept to victory, gaining 330 of the 650 seats to secure an overall majority. They did this by attracting 36.8% of votes cast, some 3.2% more than the opinion polls had predicted.

It is worth bearing in mind, therefore, that—in effect—those 3.2% of voters decided the result of the election. Had half of them voted differently, there would likely have been a hung parliament. When you consider turnout, you could even suggest that *fewer than one per cent of the registered electorate* decided the ultimate outcome, prevented a hung parliament, and guaranteed—against all odds—that a Brexit referendum would take place.

A similar picture emerges with the referendum itself. A total of 17.4 million people voted for Leave, compared to 16.1 million who voted for Remain. The margin, some 1.3 million votes, equates to around 2% of the total population of the United Kingdom. Had half of these people—that is, 1% of the UK population—voted differently, then Remain would have won.

None of this is to say that democratic elections and referenda are anything other than valid. Their results may be close, with chance elements proving crucial, but close results are just as democratic as any other. The point here is that in the story of Brexit, tiny details ended up making enormous differences. To claim that the result was somehow inevitable seems quite far-fetched. It follows, then, that the proposition that Brexit was predestined by the fall of the British Empire is equally far-fetched. The precise opposite outcome—that is, no Brexit at all—could easily have emerged from almost identical circumstances.

In other words, when we fully focus on the improbability of events, the complexity of small details, and the role of chance, it is very hard to sustain a claim that Brexit flowed inexorably from imperial demise.

The Problem of Easily Remembered Examples

Commentators who argue that Brexit can be traced (even in part) to the fall of empire have provided many examples to justify their ideas. But sometimes these examples appear convincing simply because we recognise them. Research into the psychology of reasoning has suggested that we attach undue importance to information we can easily remember. Psychologists refer to this habit as the 'availability heuristic.' When forming conclusions, we take mental shortcuts (referred to as 'heuristics') based on how readily an example springs to mind (in other words, how 'available' it is).

If we can remember an idea or event, we immediately see it as more significant than something that is difficult to recall. In other words, we fail to control for the fact that we don't know everything.

Mental shortcuts of this kind greatly affect the choices people make, especially when they are under stress. In Chapter 2, we will look at many other 'heuristics', and how they affect the Brexit choices of voters, negotiators, and politicians.

When asked about British history, most people immediately think of political history. Political history deals with governments, the affairs of state, the influence of leaders, and major diplomatic events such as wars. Few people think about social history, which deals with the history of everyday life, such as what childhood was like in the past, how women were treated, or how families and communities interacted with each other. Even fewer people think about intellectual history, such as the history of 'race' as an idea, or past attitudes towards the role of evidence in evaluating knowledge. Nonetheless, it is reasonable to suggest that these types of histories are just as important as political history in explaining the emergence of contemporary views.

From schoolbooks to banknotes to surnames to food, never mind art and literature, reminders of empire are ubiquitous in British society. Equally conspicuous is the fact that the British Empire no longer exist, that it is a truly historical thing. The claim that the demise of empire is influential on today's politics is given extra weight by the very familiarity of post-imperial cues in daily life. However, familiarity with its broader elements should not determine whether a theory is believed. Just because something is easy to remember does not mean that it is relevant.

The Problem of Counterexamples

To most people, providing examples feels like a good way to attempt to prove an argument. However, it is not a very scientific way. In fact, one of the simplest techniques of scientific reasoning is not to look for examples—but instead to look for *counterexamples*. This relates to the overall notion of *falsification*. A scientific idea is more useful if it is phrased in a way that is falsifiable, and more progress will be made in generating knowledge if you attempt to falsify it.

We can all see that Britain once had an empire and that its people voted to leave the European Union. However, examples will not prove cause-and-effect. Counterexamples, on the other hand, are much more powerful. A clear counterexample will effectively disprove a cause-and-effect theory. For example, like Britain, France once had an empire, but even its most Eurosceptic politicians no longer propose that the French people should vote for Frexit. If being a former imperial power is a key reason why British voters chose to leave the European Union, then why is the same thing not happening in France?

Similarly, Spain once had a colonial empire, as did Portugal, Belgium, and the Netherlands. Arguably, so did Denmark, Italy, Germany, and even Sweden. All these countries could be said to be in a similar position to Britain. Their glory days as imperial powers are long over, and, in relative terms, their status in the world today is significantly reduced. Yet in these countries, calls to exit the European Union are confined to the furthest fringes of politics.

Of course, all these places are different, and their imperial experiences just might not be the same as Britain's. The United Kingdom might be a special case. We should also remember that political events are multi-causal. But as a quick take on the problem, we can note that several *potential* counterexamples do in fact exist. Therefore, even at their simplest, claims that the fall of the British Empire accounts for Brexit are diminished. At the very least, things are more complicated than that.

The Problem of Simpler Explanations

A final principle of scientific reasoning relates to the dangers of over-elaboration. We refer to this principle as 'parsimony', the idea that simpler explanations are always more logically defensible than complex ones. In some ways, the claim that the demise of the British Empire caused Brexit is a very simple explanation. However, in the context of scientific reasoning, we consider the 'simplest' explanation to be the one that relies on the fewest contingencies, or the one that makes the fewest uncorroborated assumptions. In other words, it is the one that leaves least to chance.

Did the British people vote for Brexit because of a deep-seated, even unconscious, sentiment relating to intergenerational humiliation at the hands of an unappreciative outside world, and because of the residual effects of imperial decline, a process that many historians say began in the late nineteenth century? Or did the British people vote for Brexit because, on the date of the referendum, a majority of them felt that their self-interest would be served by doing so?

By any reckoning, the latter explanation is the more parsimonious. We know that a majority of voters voted for Brexit on referendum day. We know, generally, that voters are motivated to cast votes that serve their own interests (or, put another way, we know that they are motivated to *avoid* casting votes that they believe will *damage* their interests). Neither of these assumptions is tentative.

However, we do *not* know whether an appreciable portion of the electorate was motivated by the post-imperial anxieties of British culture.

Admittedly, some voters may have equated this with their own self-interests, choosing to vote Leave on post-imperial grounds. However, specifying the nature of voters' perceived self-interests is more tentative than not specifying it. Therefore, an overall explanation that invokes post-imperial anxiety will be less parsimonious than one that does not.

The biggest problem with the psychodrama approach is the very fact that it is dramatic. Drama stems from detail. The more details you see in a theory, the more seductive it becomes. Also, a detailed theory is more memorable than a dull theory, which, because of the availability heuristic, makes it seem more significant. However, more details also mean more points of weakness. In a detailed theory, in which several elements are unproven, any one that turns out to be unreliable will bring the entire house of cards crashing down.

An elaborate theory can, of course, be correct. But in the absence of proof that it is, we cannot say so for sure. In that event, and all other things being equal, a simpler alternative theory will always be more logically defensible.

The Brexit-as-post-imperial-psychodrama theory might be many things. But simple it certainly is not.

The Real Psychology of Brexit

The psychodrama theory of Brexit—where Brexit represents 'the last vestiges of empire working their way out of the British psyche' (with some sadomasochism thrown in for good measure)—is colourful, imaginative, and thought-provoking. It offers many talking points and raises important questions. However, as a psychological account, it has several limitations. One is that it is not particularly scientific. The psychodrama approach has its place, but a more scientific approach has a place too. After all, reliable, evidence-based knowledge will surely prove more useful in the long run than knowledge of the unreliable, speculative kind.

The advantages of scientific psychology are not just methodological. They are also ethical. Without an active effort to accumulate evidence, to circumvent bias, and to test claims for falsifiability, there will be an ever-present danger of being lulled by explanations that simply tell us what we want to hear.

Sometimes, commentators invoke ideas of empire to indicate their support for Brexit. They argue that Brexit is merely the latest in a long line of British global conquests. The inherent over-simplification of this narrative threatens to make Brexit 'look easy,' perhaps helping to fool British negotiators into falsely assuming that other countries will fall into line and accept their imperial demands (Lis, 2019).

However, in most cases, it is Remain-oriented commentators who link Brexit to empire. The connotations are clear. Leave voters are dinosaurs, racists, and monomaniacs, forever hankering after a long-gone monocultural and hierarchical past, uncomfortable in the modern world and its diversity and egalitarianism. These post-imperial, post-colonial, sadopopulist Leave supporters operate incorrigibly beyond mainstream standards of reason. They xenophobically chant 'Go back where you came from' at foreigners, when in fact it is *they* who yearn to go back in time to where it is *they* came from: to romantic, colonialist, imperial, beautiful England (Earle, 2017).

But if this gloomy caricature is propelled by a psychodrama theory that itself is unsupportable, then we must ask whether it is all just another example of Brexit propaganda. The post-imperial psychodrama not only casts a slur on Leave supporters, it also portrays Remainers in an excessively flattering light. It implies that they are somehow immune to the legacies of colonialism, as though they never avail of white privilege and are incapable of holding post-imperialist views. Postcolonialism, it seems, is something that happens to other people—the ones who support Brexit.

The psychodrama approach is also limited in its reductionism. It perpetuates polarisation. It glosses over the fact that Brexit is supported by anticolonialists on the extreme-left, as well politicians on the extreme right. It ignores the fact that Brexit is supported by significant numbers of black and minority-ethnic citizens—who presumably *don't* hanker after the glory days of the British Empire. Ideas relating to identity, culture, race, language, communities, and religion are all psychologically important, but positing a post-imperial narrative reduces everything to a disappointingly binary scheme: the sophisticates who are comfortable in the modern world, versus the primitives who can't get their heads around it.

Finding ways to better understand Brexit is important for many reasons. The most clichéd is that we can learn from the past, avoid repeating our mistakes, and build a better future. From a psychological perspective, issues of mental health and well-being are also salient. The psychodrama approach draws attention away from the quite serious toll that Brexit's social disruption will place on mental health in Britain. Ironically, it does so by erroneously pathologising people's political preferences. In fact, the way that post-imperial narratives serve to console Remainers while demonising Leavers suggests that these worldviews are actually a *symptom* of mass anxiety, rather than a suitable basis from which to try to explain it. Imperial narratives require attention, but mainly because they lead people to misunderstand the nature of Brexit stress. We will examine this impact of Brexit on mental health in Chapter 4.

There is a final reason why it is important to unpack the post-imperial psychodrama of Brexit. Linking Brexit to post-imperial malaise depicts current events as driven by long-range historical influence. It overlooks the fact that many major events are contingent on recent decisions, current attitudes, and present-day actions. In other words, if events like Brexit are caused by falling empires, there would appear to be little that ordinary people can do to influence them. In reality, however, events like Brexit result from factors that are far more mundane. This, in turn, should mean that we have greater power to intervene. Psychology suggests that we have this power. Psychodrama, by contrast, is disempowering.

Far from being written by history, Brexit is an ongoing cultural event shaped by psychological choices, social forces, and the human capacity for reason. The way people view their world, prioritise their needs, and formulate their decisions is integral to understanding Brexit, and to predicting its course. In Brexit lore there is much talk about 'the will of the British people.' It is to this notion of British will—the psychology of political reason—that we shall now turn.

2

Reasoning Through Brexit

I. Decisions, Decisions

In an ideal world, referendums constitute a form of 'direct democracy'. On planet Brexit, however, democracy might be a lot of things, but one thing you would never call it is 'direct'.

Perhaps it is no surprise, therefore, that the United Kingdom tends to avoid holding referendums at all. The British political tradition sees parliament, rather than the people, as sovereign. No court can overrule parliament. No parliament can pass a law that a future parliament can't change.

In classically imperial tones, the British even consider their nation to be the 'mother of parliaments.' They believe other countries' governments could stand to learn a thing or two from the British approach.

If all else fails, turn to parliament.

Mother, after all, knows best.

It is true that some countries hold more referendums than others. Switzerland, for example, holds around ten referendums per year. But while British referendums are unusual, they are by no means rare. In the two decades leading up to Brexit, the United Kingdom held nine major referendums, an average of around one referendum every twenty-six months.

© The Author(s) 2019
B. M. Hughes, *The Psychology of Brexit*,
https://doi.org/10.1007/978-3-030-29364-2_2

Many of these plebiscites related to local devolution, and were conducted regionally. Nonetheless, every part of the United Kingdom enjoyed the experience multiple times.

The people of Scotland, Wales, London, and northeast England were each asked if they wanted to be governed by devolved administrations. The Welsh were later consulted to see if they wished to strengthen their local assembly. Northern Irish voters were asked about their support for the Good Friday Agreement. Scottish voters went to the polls once more, this time to decide whether to become fully independent. And in a nationwide UK referendum, all British voters were given the chance to express their view on a proposed new system for electing MPs.

Devolution. Independence. Peace. A new electoral system. The issues put before the people certainly varied. So too did the people's reactions. While some of these referendums turned out to be highly contentious, others captured few imaginations.

Nonetheless, a common thread ran through them all. When it came to structure, as opposed to substance, these ballots were very consistent.

In all eight referendums, citizens were asked to decide between two responses: a box marked 'Yes' or one marked 'No.' Millions upon millions of such votes were cast, but every single one of them was a 'Yes' or a 'No'.

That was until June 23, 2016. For the Brexit referendum, things changed. Votes were cast in a distinctive way. This time the British people placed slightly different voting papers into their ballot boxes.

Brexit, as in so many other respects, was destined to be a special case.

That Is the Question

When first proposed, the Brexit referendum question *was* to be of a 'Yes-No' format. The government's European Union Referendum Act envisaged that voters be asked the following:

Should the United Kingdom remain a member of the European Union?

Responses, as before, were to be 'Yes' or 'No'. However, after evaluating the matter, the United Kingdom's Electoral Commission decided to alter the wording. It would now become:

Should the United Kingdom remain a member of the European Union or leave the European Union?

This newly worded question required differently phrased responses. Instead of choosing 'Yes' or 'No', voters would now have to decide between boxes labelled 'Remain a member of the European Union' or 'Leave the European Union'.

And thus, the tribal nomenclature of Remain-vs.-Leave was born.

These key words, 'Remain' and 'Leave', were selected for their neutrality. They would go on to become two of the most emotionally charged labels ever coined in British political history.

The reason for the change was subtle, but deliberate, and inarguably partisan. While the Electoral Commission had issued an open call for submissions, they received far more concerted input from pro-Brexit campaigners (Green, 2017).

These campaigners believed that a 'Yes-No' question could induce conformity in the electorate. Voters would be predisposed to comply with whatever they construed was the 'positive' thing to do. In the Scottish independence referendum, these campaigners believed, the government had suffered an unfair disadvantage in having to ask people to vote 'No'. People don't like to be negative. And it is hard to get more negative than 'No'.

In psychology, researchers refer to the 'Yes' preference as 'acquiescence bias.' It is a particularly pernicious problem for psychologists who design opinion surveys. People just like saying 'Yes'.

The impulse is unlikely to overwhelm anyone whose views are strongly held. However, for people struggling to make up their minds, its effects can be quite pernicious. When people are asked whether they agree with a statement that they are not quite sure about, the will tend to say 'Yes'. When the same statement is later rephrased in the negative and they are asked about it a second time, they will tend to say 'Yes' again.

Research in psychology suggests that undecided respondents are much more likely to affirm than disavow.

Private polling had suggested that more voters would vote to withdraw from the European Union if they were asked to endorse 'Leave' instead of ticking a box marked 'No'. Therefore, the pro-Brexit campaign made co-ordinated efforts to convince the Electoral Commission to rephrase its referendum question in order to avoid this effect (Shipman, 2016).

The Electoral Commission reported that its call for submissions had received 'clearer views' from Brexit campaigners, and advised that the 'Yes-No' format should be ditched. It would encourage voters 'to consider one response more favourably than the other,' the commission said, while a 'Remain-Leave' layout would prove to be 'more neutral' (Electoral Commission, 2015).

After a long run of 'Yes-No' referendums, the United Kingdom was now, finally, going to reconfigure its ballot papers in an attempt to circumvent a quirk of human reasoning. The psychology of choice-selection was recognised as warranting attention. Acquiescence bias might affect only a small subset of voters. However, in a close-run referendum, a small group can end up making a very big difference.

The Age of Ill-Reason

Of course, nothing is ever perfect. Some commentators thought that 'Remain-Leave' was no more neutral than 'Yes-No.' After all, 'Remain' suggested passivity, while 'Leave' was action-oriented. Maybe undecided voters would be swayed by this instead, preferring dynamism over inertia.

Psychologists have conducted lots of research on 'Yes-No' questions. But they have little to fall back on when it comes to evaluating things like 'Remain-Leave.' It is hard to be sure that 'Remain-Leave' was truly neutral. The wording was bespoke to the Brexit referendum, and concocted for a single use. That novelty alone could be said to have presented a risk. In employing an untested format, the referendum was taking a step into the unknown.

The design of the ballot paper also attracted criticism. The 'Remain' option took up more space on the page. After all, 'Remain a member of the European Union' was a longer phrase than 'Leave the European Union'. It required more ink. Did this make the 'Remain' option look more substantial? Does size matter if you are a fickle undecided voter?

One politician complained that the word 'Leave' appeared too close to the centre of the page. It was much closer to the middle than the word 'Remain'. He said that this would influence voters to choose 'Leave' because it ensured the word appeared in people's eyelines as soon as they gazed upon their ballots. He pointed out that this exact ploy was used by Hitler, no less, in 1938, when rigging a referendum on the proposed annexation of Austria. In fact, according to him, the Brexit ballot paper was 'worse than the Hitler ballot paper,' because it was 'subliminal' (Crisp, 2016).

These ergonomic features might seem inconsequential, and most media reporting dismissed them as such. However, from a psychological perspective, they are difficult to entirely ignore. Human beings do not always make considered choices having weighed up the available evidence. Nor do they voluntarily opt out of decision-making just because they are poorly informed. The fickleness of their voting choices should not be underestimated.

The psychology of human reasoning suggests that, in many situations, people incline toward impulsive, irrational, and inexplicable decisions. They do so when they are under time pressure, when they are emotional, and when they are faced with ambiguity. That particular combination of circumstances will sound extremely familiar to anyone who follows Brexit.

Surveys conducted just after the 2016 referendum showed that one-in-ten voters did not make a voting decision until the day of the referendum itself (Ashcroft, 2016). They literally rocked up to the polling station with an open mind. Who knows what determined their final decisions, as they stood alone in the polling booths, their pencils aloft, gazing at the fresh voting papers before them.

They did not have canvassers whispering in their ears, or campaign leaflets in their hands to read. They were undecided when they arrived but now faced a moment of reckoning. Memories of a tumultuous referendum campaign swirled in their minds, all the pros and cons, all the good and the bad, all the exciting and the depressing claims they had heard. What was it to be? 'Remain' or 'Leave'? They had to decide. There would be no more procrastinating. Crunch time had arrived.

One-in-ten voters equates to three million votes. In the end, just over one million votes separated Remain from Leave. The possibility that a decisive portion of the electorate made their voting choices on impulse, under time pressure, while stressed, and with ambiguous conviction, does not seem at all that far-fetched.

The complexity of the subsequent Brexit negotiations, their electoral fallout, and the resultant collapse of the traditional British party political system suggests that time pressure, emotion, and ambiguity continue to cause disarray. Their destructive effect on decision-making continues to be felt.

Psychological research helps us to understand why human minds find these challenges very difficult. Our ultimate choices are rarely that forensic. Even those Brexit voters who made up their minds *prior* to polling day will have done so while hampered by the limitations of human reasoning.

Human minds are just very poorly designed for dealing with things like Brexit.

Brexit Means…

In Chapter 1, we discussed how human brains are liable to impose meaning on the meaningless. Our brains are pattern-detecting engines. They are uncomfortable with ambiguity. When we encounter something ambiguous, we presume to know what it signifies. We convince ourselves that we understand it.

Brexit, to put it mildly, is exceedingly ambiguous. And so it is no surprise that millions of people purport to know what it is. They know, for example, that they want it.

If anything, the ambiguity of Brexit *enhances* its popularity. By definition, it broadens its appeal. Different audiences with different interests can all claim to want Brexit, and to want it now.

For some, Brexit means national liberation for the United Kingdom and a confident expression of autonomy. For others, it is Britain's safety strategy, a way to avoid becoming entangled by risky economic misadventures of foreign governments. For others, it is a chance to extricate Britain from the neocapitalist world order and its military-industrial complex. For still others it is a logical attempt to undo the negative economic changes that have afflicted them during the period of EU membership. And for others it is a way of preserving Britishness, lest it become diluted by multiculturalism.

For even others it means freedom from red tape, intrusive regulation, and nanny-statism. And for others it is a way of renouncing mainstream politics, punishing those elites who deign to feel superior, and rejecting, as of right, a predetermined template for political progress that they feel has been foisted upon them.

The common theme is that Brexit signifies change. All interpretations of Brexit involve a rejection of the status quo. 'Leave' involves 'leaving' the present, rejecting your circumstances as you find them. By contrast, 'Remain' involves staying put, accepting that things should 'remain' the way they are.

Defining Brexit as 'change' makes people more likely to support it. After all, to object to change is to imply that everything is fine as it is. In reality, very few people would take that view. So when Brexit is depicted as change—albeit vague, ill-defined, and possibly counterproductive change—people are gravitationally drawn to support it.

The underlying psychological pull comes from the availability heuristic, that mental shortcut we discussed in Chapter 1. This relates to the presumed significance attached to easily remembered information. Everyone can think of examples of things that need to be changed. It is easier to identify what updates are required than to articulate what should be left alone. Because of the availability heuristic, calls for change feel more significant and more convincing than calls for stability.

Offering to be a 'change agent' is heroic and memorable. Offering to be 'strong and stable' is a much tougher sell.

Inside the bubble of political implementation, there are many more meanings for Brexit. The referendum wording offered a blankish canvass, going no further than to say that Britain should 'leave the European Union.' There was no direct reference to Britain's relationship with the single market, the customs union, the European Court of Justice, or with entities such as Euratom, the European Medicines Agency, or the European Banking Authority.

Some countries, such as Norway and Switzerland, have never been members of the European Union, yet are enmeshed in many of its activities. Therefore, the United Kingdom could 'leave the European Union' but still remain a member of, say, the European single market. Nonetheless, as is widely discussed, British government policy has been to withdraw from every institution that could conceivably be said to comprise the EU, including those that other non-EU member states are happily involved in.

Many pro-Brexit campaigners are firmly committed to this absolutist interpretation. Many others are not. Brexit, as always, is characterised by its ambiguity.

But change is a double-edged aspiration. To yearn for change is more than to express a belief in optimistic possibilities. It is to acknowledge that all is not well with your current predicament. To crave change intensely is to signal a type of despair. The ambiguity of Brexit provides many voters with an outlet for outrage.

Their call for change is really a cry for help.

This Message Will Self-Destruct...

In Chapter 1, we noted how Brexit attitudes are often pathologised. One of the most frequent ways this happens is when Brexit is described as a form of 'self-harm.'

The term has been used repeatedly. In an impassioned speech, former Prime Minister John Major decried Brexit as a 'policy of self-harm' that would systematically hurt 'those who have the least' (Merrick, 2019). Another former Prime Minister, Gordon Brown, agreed, claiming that Leavers were turning an 'act of economic self-harm into a test of patriotism' (Quinn, 2019). Chancellor of the Exchequer Philip Hammond warned that a no-deal Brexit, in particular, would create 'economic self-harm' (Hills, 2019).

Irish Prime Minister and qualified medical doctor Leo Varadkar confirmed the overall diagnosis. According to him, Brexit is 'a real act of self-harm' that has 'not been fully thought through' (Randerson, 2019).

Former Conservative Party chairman Chris Patten declared Brexit 'an act of egregious self-harm' (Manley, 2018). To Live Aid founder Bob Geldof, it was 'the greatest act of national self-harm that has ever been perpetrated in British history' (Nair, 2017). Former Liberal Democrats leader Paddy Ashdown described Brexit as 'a monumental act of self-harm,' which he said would 'bewilder historians' (Ashdown, 2017).

But perhaps not all historians. British academic Ian Kershaw, widely considered one of the world's leading experts on Hitler, seemed relatively unbewildered. In an interview, he agreed that Brexit is 'the greatest act of self-harm by any major country' since Germany's descent into Nazi dictatorship (Eaton, 2018).

Any case of self-harm is, of course, profound and troubling. Self-harm is a worryingly common mental health problem. In the United Kingdom alone, research suggests that up to one-in-six adults under the age of 35 have self-harmed during their lives, with one-in-ten women under the age of 23 having done so in the past year. Eighty per cent of young adults who self-harm do so more than once (O'Connor et al., 2018). Contrary to widespread belief, self-harm is rarely an effort to attract attention. Most people who harm themselves go to great effort to conceal the fact. For many, self-harm is a desperate attempt to cope with overwhelming mental pain.

With Brexit, the comparison with 'self-harm' implies that people who engage in it are irrational. It suggests they must be stopped—not precisely for their own benefit, of course, but in order to prevent innocent bystanders (and especially Remainers) from being swept up in collateral damage. Self-harm is seen as another symptom of the psychopathology of Leave supporters, another sign of their insanity.

The use of self-harm as a handy metaphor for condemning Brexit raises some troubling questions about public attitudes to mental health and the accuracy of cultural depictions of suffering.

It is for economists to consider whether Brexit, whatever form it takes, will precipitate actual economic harm. Psychologists, on the other hand, can help adjudicate the core cognitive point. Is it truly irrational for people to support Brexit, given the likely economic consequences?

Or is there a wider explicable logic for Brexit supporters to want to leave the European Union? And if there is, why are opponents of Brexit so unable to recognise and acknowledge it?

These questions lie at the very heart of the psychology of Brexit.

It's (Not) the Economy, Stupid

While it is indeed for economists to consider whether Brexit will damage the economy, there is no doubt that this is their widely held view. However, only a tiny minority of British voters are economists.

Therefore, the task for psychologists is to assess how the vast bulk of British voters came to make up their minds—and how, given the narrative of self-harm, around half of them decided to support their country's withdrawal from the European Union.

One way to approach the issue is to look for circumstantial factors that might prompt people to back Brexit. For example, at first glance, it would seem there is a strong link between poverty and Brexit support.

A number of researchers have focused on survey statistics gathered by the British Election Study. The BES is a project that has been collating data on UK elections since the 1960s. The dataset relating to Brexit contains survey responses from over 31,000 voters, which, as these things go, is a very large sample. When the numbers have been crunched, it seems that people living in poor households are much more likely to support Brexit than those living in wealthy ones. Support for leaving the European Union is around 58% in homes with incomes less than £20,000, compared to only 35% in those where incomes exceed £60,000 (Goodwin & Heath, 2016).

Similar analyses also suggest that older British voters are more likely to support Brexit than younger ones. At the time of the referendum, around 60% of voters over 65 voted Leave, compared to just 30% of voters under the age of 25. Two years later, this age difference had widened. Brexit support in the over-65s had increased to 66%, while for the under-25s, it had fallen to 18% (Curtice, 2018).

Another likely factor is education. Several analyses have shown that people with fewer educational qualifications are more likely to be Brexit supporters. For example, for the local authority areas of England, the percentage of residents who hold at least a Level 4 qualification (a Higher National Certificate) closely mirrors its Brexit vote. Areas with more qualified residents contain fewer Brexit supporters, while places where few people are qualified are more likely to vote Leave. In statistical language, the association between education and Leave-votes equates to an 'R-squared' of 0.8 (Rae, 2016). This means that around 80% of people's decision to support Brexit can be 'explained'—statistically speaking—by their education level.

However, one problem with this type of information is that all these factors—income, age, and education—are intertwined. They affect each other. Therefore, when one of them looks to be driving Brexit, it could be one of the others that is really doing so.

Take, for example, education and age. In the United Kingdom, there has been a massive increase in university participation over the past thirty years. As a result, younger British adults are more likely to have degrees than older ones. The difference in Brexit attitudes between older and younger adults could really be due to the effects of education. Younger voters might dislike Brexit not because they are *young*, but because they have been to university. Education has turned them against Brexit—age doesn't come into it.

Alternatively, maybe it's the other way around. Maybe the age difference in Brexit attitudes makes it *look like* there is an education difference. Perhaps people with degrees are less likely to support Brexit because, by dint of circumstance, they happen to be younger. In reality, their view would be the same whether or not they ever went to university. Maybe *youth* is why they are against Brexit—and *education* doesn't come into it.

And don't forget poverty. Low household income is a major barrier to education. This muddies the waters even more. When we see education predicting people's views about Brexit, it could be that there is a hidden underlying effect for household income. Education level is a signifier of economic status. We can use education level to classify people as 'rich' or 'poor'. Facing poverty could be the reason some people have fewer qualifications, while also—separately—causing them to support Brexit.

Once again, this could work the other way. After all, in many occupations, education level is a determinant of salary. People with higher qualifications are likely to earn more. If we see that poverty is linked to Brexit, it could be that *differences in education* are driving the effects. *Having fewer qualifications* could explain *why some people face poverty*, while also—separately—causing them to support Brexit.

Because of the type of data they study, psychologists frequently encounter this problem. They often have lots of bits of interwoven information. The challenge is to figure out which factors are key to explaining the outcomes, which ones are somewhere in the mix but playing a peripheral part, and which ones look relevant but are not really relevant at all.

The good news is that psychologists can use a statistical technique called 'regression' to compare and contrast the various factors. This helps to sort out their comparative importance. When statistical regression is used to examine age, income, and education levels at the same time, it turns out that education level is by far the strongest predictor of Brexit attitudes. In other words, even when you take income and age into account, differences in education still cause big differences in views about Brexit.

Researchers working on that big dataset from the British Election Study showed that support for Brexit among voters who left education after secondary school is around 30 percentage points higher than among voters who completed university (Goodwin & Heath, 2016). This was true *regardless of people's ages*, and *regardless of their incomes*.

It seems that dropping out of education early really does make people more attracted to Brexit.

Silver-Medal Anxiety

Psychology research can help explain why. Researchers who study consumer choices have identified an effect that they explain under the umbrella term of 'prospect theory' (Tversky & Kahneman, 1992). Prospect theory describes how people compare costs and benefits, taking account of what they think will happen in the future (their 'prospects').

The crucial point is that people weight costs differently to how they weight benefits. The pain of a cost is felt more than the satisfaction of an equivalent benefit.

A person who finds a ten-pound note on the street feels happier than a person who finds *two* ten-pound notes but then *loses* one of them shortly afterwards. Both people have gained ten pounds, and so technically both have similar benefits. However, the second person feel bad because losses are always felt more than equivalent gains.

Similarly, athletes who win bronze medals are often happier than those who get silver. Silver medallists focus on what they have lost, whereas bronze medallists focus on how close they were to winning nothing. Because the emotions associated with costs are felt more acutely than those arising from benefits, the cost-benefit analysis of silver medallists skews negatively. Silver medallists are tormented by the pain of losing out on gold, while bronze medallists feel nothing but the joy for simply having reached the podium.

Sports fans have observed this difference for many years. Psychologists themselves have made Olympian efforts to research the matter. In one study, they scrutinised reams of press photographs of judo competitors at the precise moment they won, or missed out on, a medal (Matsumoto & Willingham, 2006). They found that the spontaneous smiles of athletes who won bronze medals were more emotionally 'authentic' than the forced expressions produced by athletes who discovered they were getting silvers. (Psychologists, you will be pleased to learn, have a formal method of classifying smiles for authenticity.)

Prospect theory also tells us something about how people approach risk: if they rate their future prospects as poor, they are much more likely to gamble in an effort to avoid cost. In other words, if a person feels secure, they will be risk-averse—but if they feel insecure, they will accept risk more readily. When you have little to lose, you might as well take a few chances.

This explains why people in dire circumstances often take greater risks. Consumers who run up debts will often spend more, rather than less, on lottery tickets. Patients who are severely ill will be more likely to volunteer for experimental medical treatments. And people who feel disconnected from mainstream society become more likely to vote for extremists.

The important thing to remember is that prospect theory focuses on *perceived* prospects rather than material outcomes, or indeed current material well-being. The silver medallist is technically better off than the bronze medallist, but they still feel worse. Prospect theory suggests that support for Brexit may result from the fact that many people in Britain feel their future prospects are poor, relative to their current situation.

People who leave education early could be said to have weaker economic prospects than those who don't. Therefore, the statistical link between education level and Brexit makes sense in terms of prospect theory. It is certainly a seductive narrative. But remember, we should not get carried away by seductive narratives.

Our evidence, thus far, is circumstantial. For one thing, there appear to be many falsifying examples—all the political leaders, writers, and other highly qualified people who publicly support Brexit.

An interesting finding from the British Election Study may help to bolster our suspicions. The researchers found an 'interaction' between education levels and geography. In statistical language, an interaction is where two factors work together to exert a joint causal effect on an outcome. In this case, the researchers found that people with educational qualifications feel differently about Brexit depending on what part of the country they live in.

People with degrees are more likely to support Brexit if they live in an area *where very few other people have degrees*. In other words, while graduates are statistically more likely to reject Brexit, graduates who live in low-skilled communities are more likely to vote like non-graduates (Goodwin & Heath, 2016).

This is consistent with prospect theory. In general, graduates who live in low-skilled neighbourhoods are unlikely to have as many opportunities as graduates who live in high-skilled ones. Despite having degrees, they have fewer chances to use these qualifications within their own locale. Having gone to university does not over-ride the fact that their immediate prospects are less promising than those of people who live in more prosperous areas. These diminished prospects make them less risk-averse.

By extension, it should not matter how poor or wealthy a person is. Anyone can feel that their future prospects are negative. Bus drivers might worry about the effects of job market competition on salary levels. Teachers might worry about the impact of demographic changes on job security. Middle-class pensioners might worry about the impact of inflation on the value of savings. Business owners might worry about the sustainability of profits in the face of international competition.

For anyone who feels their prospects are not what they should be, it becomes rational to consider Brexit a reasonable proposition. After all, why not take the chance? Everything just might work out, and if it doesn't, well, in terms of your personal prospects, little will change. You can't lose what you don't have.

Complex Numbers

Of course, much of this comes down to perception—*perceived* costs, *perceived* benefits, and *perceived* risks. Perception, by definition, resides permanently in the eye of the beholder. Prospect theory might help to explain some of the key trends. But it does not paint the full psychological picture.

We should remember, for example, that views about Brexit are very finely balanced. The majority in the 2016 referendum was slight. According to opinion polls, little has changed in subsequent years. The aggregate opinion may have shifted from Leave towards Remain, but the margin is still very small (Curtice, 2018). The best we can say is that around half the people support Brexit and around half do not. Any psychological factors that affect opinion will do so in subtle ways.

Prospect theory is pertinent here too. In opinion polls, costs and benefits are hypothetical. In referendums, they are real. Prospect theory suggests that people will approach real referendums differently to opinion polls. It is one of the main reasons opinion polls find it difficult to capture real-world voting intentions. They fail to account for the distorting effects of real-world risk-aversion.

Socioeconomic deprivation is a pernicious social problem that drives many to despair. But the claim that Brexit is propelled purely by poverty or lack of education is misleading. The Brexit referendum vote cut across the socioeconomic strata. Large numbers of affluent people from economically secure communities voted Leave. In fact, the outcome of the referendum was largely dependent on them (Dorling, 2016). Most of the political leaders who support Brexit today are conspicuously wealthy and, by any measure, very well educated.

Brexit resembles self-harm, or nihilism, only if you adopt an economic norm. To many people, it holds other attractions. For example, national and social identity often override economic considerations. This is an important theme that we will discuss in Chapter 3. The main point here is that perceptions of reality are far more influential than reality itself. This is key to the psychology of Brexit. In fact, it is key to the psychology of most things in life.

The psychology of Brexit suggests that support for Leave is not as irrational as it is often made out to be. But that is not to say that irrationality doesn't come into things. In fact, the problem of irrationality appears all over the Brexit landscape—and not just on the Leave side. The notion that people in general approach political questions with clear-headed reason is itself an irrational belief. The idea that only *some* people are irrational—primarily those people who disagree with you on political matters—is a second dangerous misconception.

Remainers are just as likely as Leavers to vote with their hearts instead of their heads. They are just as likely to labour under erroneous misapprehensions regarding key social concerns like immigration flows and poverty levels. And they are just as liable to view the United Kingdom, its society, and its true place in the world through a postcolonial lens.

Remain does not have a monopoly on reason.

This is because Remainers are human beings.

A mistake we often make is to assume that human reasoning is, by default, rational. In culture, we classify humanity itself as a rational species. Indeed the word 'rational' often has connotations that deviate from its core meaning. According to a dictionary, 'rational' means 'in accordance with logic'. According to a thesaurus, it means things like 'sensible', 'mentally sound', or 'sane.'

In reality, it is perfectly normal for human beings to make choices, even important ones, that are unclear, imprudent, or wrong-headed. It happens all the time. It is how our brains work. And it is why politics operates in the way that it does.

Democracy is founded on the premise that people typically are rational. Politics is founded on the premise that most often they typically are not.

II. A Brain Made for Taking Shortcuts

As described in Chapter 1, humans frequently take mental shortcuts when dealing with complex information. The availability heuristic—where we attach significance to details that we can remember easily—is a good example. There is nothing inherently wrong with mental shortcuts, or 'heuristics.' Most of the time, the information we remember easily just *is* the most significant. It makes sense for us to assume that it is. It is an efficient use of brainpower.

Were we to approach every situation in life as though we were encountering it for the first time, and then try to analyse every detail as though we had never seen it before, we would find ordinary life very difficult. We would be overwhelmed by the millions of points of detail we see, hear, and have to think about every day.

Most of life is cyclical. We encounter most situations in different forms several times. If on each occasion we had to analyse from first principles all the elements of a situation, we wouldn't be able to function. The most effective biological organisms will learn to re-enact behaviours that they can apply, repeatedly, to common situations. Human psychology is shaped by natural selection. Our habits of thought—and our ability to take mental shortcuts—is a skill that we use to survive, to reproduce, and, ultimately, to evolve.

The problem, of course, is the error rate. Mental shortcuts might give us the right answer most of the time, but some of the time it will give us the opposite. This is why in politics, marketing, and other forms of professional persuasion, the ability to appeal to people's mental shortcuts is often more effective than rational argument.

For psychologists, Brexit is a giant real-time case study in which mental shortcuts, and their distorting consequences, are extravagantly on display.

We can classify these mental shortcuts into broadly three groups: *rules of thumb*; *peer pressure effects*; and *problems of rose-tinted glasses*. In the coming pages we will consider examples from each of these three groups, and the part they all have played in producing the Brexit saga.

Rules of Thumb: Free-Flowing Memories

Through countless experiments and surveys, psychologists have uncovered dozens of rules of thumb that humans commonly apply to everyday decision-making. The **availability heuristic** we described earlier is one of the most powerful. It drives us to draw false conclusions simply on the basis of how easy it is to remember something. It helps explain why people come to believe that the EU looms large in their lives, that immigration is a threat, and that mainstream politicians are not to be trusted.

The classic classroom example is to ask students what they think is more common: English-language words beginning with the letter 'k', or English-language words in which 'k' is the third letter (Tversky & Kahneman, 1973). Because it is much easier to think of words that *begin* with a particular letter, most students conclude that words beginning with 'k' are more prevalent. In reality, there are three times as many words in English that contain 'k' as the third letter. Just because something is easy to remember does not mean that there is more of it about.

People can end up believing that all sorts of things are more common and impactful than they really are. For example, people usually overestimate their likelihood of being killed in a terrorist attack or murdered, because media reports often give significant attention to relatively rare occurrences—such as terrorist attacks or murders (Mitchell & Roberts, 2012). The availability heuristic leads people to the false conclusion that such events are frequent.

The irony is that rare events are often newsworthy precisely *because* they are rare. It would be unfair to criticise the media for reporting on them. However, the unfortunate side-effect of human thought habits is to make people see media attention as a kind of physical measure. If something is in the news a lot, it must be very common. If it is all over the news, *then it must be all around us.*

What people come to believe about the European Union, the effects of migration, the consequences of withdrawal, or the trustworthiness of politicians, is rarely drawn from first-hand investigation. The atmosphere of national attitudes is slowly constructed from elements of media reports.

The availability heuristic can create a dramatic gap between perception and reality. In 2013, the Royal Statistical Society conducted a large-scale survey that revealed just how wildly inaccurate were the views of the British public in the years just prior to the Brexit referendum (Ipsos MORI, 2013):

- Survey respondents reported believing that 31% of people living in the United Kingdom were immigrants. In reality, only 13% were. That's an error of a factor of three (in that their answer was around three times the correct value).
- They thought that 24% of British adults were Muslims. The correct figure is just 5%. That's an error of a factor of *five*.
- They believed that around 30% of British adults are single parents. In reality only 3% are. That's an error of a factor of *ten*.
- They thought that 15% of teenagers become pregnant each year, when only 0.6% actually do. That's an error of a factor of *twenty-five*.
- They believed that of every £100 of welfare received in Britain, £24 was being claimed fraudulently. In reality, the correct amount was 70p. That's an error of a factor of *thirty-five*.

The range of topics about which the average British person seemed utterly clueless was staggering. They thought crime was increasing when it was actually decreasing, and that the government spent more on international aid than on education or pensions, when actually the aid budget was less than one fifteenth of the education and pensions budgets.

All these issues are discussed regularly in the media. Many are the subject of frequent front pages. They are perennial hot topics, never more so than during the Brexit referendum. All in all, you would expect the public to be very knowledgeable about them. Instead, they were egregiously misinformed. The British public's understanding of the very topics they say they are interested in, if not obsessed with, could hardly have been more hopeless.

This is entirely consistent with the availability heuristic. People can't remember statistical detail, but they *can* remember that these topics made the news. The ease with which these recollections can be called to mind—their *availability*—creates a false impact. People ended up grossly overestimating the frequency of events, and the intensity of the problems they cause.

Indeed, the British public were probably *better* informed about topics that they never encountered in the news.

It is worth noting that in the United Kingdom most mainstream media, especially print media, report news in a partisan fashion. Some papers are pro-European, but many of the largest-circulation newspapers have long-held scepticism towards the EU, and sometimes towards globalisation more generally. A number are stridently pro-Brexit. In addition, British newspapers have a long-established tradition of presenting news in a visually dramatic way. Front pages are carefully designed to be eye-catching, attention-grabbing, and memorable. They are laced with sensationalist reporting.

When an Oxford University research institute analysed British newspapers during the Brexit referendum, they found that five major national newspapers carried mostly pro-Leave stories (namely, the *Daily Mail*, the *Daily Express*, the *Daily Star*, *The Sun* and the *Daily Telegraph*). Three major national newspapers were mostly pro-Remain (the *Daily Mirror*, *The Guardian*, and the *Financial Times*). Just one major daily (*The Times*) was considered to have balanced pro- and anti-Brexit coverage (although, ultimately, its editorial called upon readers to vote Remain). The net result was that 45% of the stories appearing in UK national newspapers were supportive of the Leave position, with just 27% of stories supporting Remain (Levy, Aslan, & Bironzo, 2016).

Regional newspapers in Britain are often ignored by researchers, but they are very widely read by citizens. These papers tend to cover the news quite differently to the nationals. A particular distinction is that for years they covered fewer European stories. But when Brexit burst on the scene, Europe stories became unavoidable. Statistical studies show that there was a steady increase in EU-related coverage in regional newspapers for a year prior to the referendum. Importantly, regional newspapers were much more likely than national papers to report negative stories about immigrants (Walter, 2019).

Recall that the availability heuristic gives people the false impression that newsworthy events are common. When readers observe voluminous coverage of the EU and its migrants, they will likely come to believe that the associated problems are much more pertinent—and far more frequent—than they are in reality.

There are many studies that look at how the media report on Brexit. The availability heuristic should bring such research into very sharp relief. Following what flows through the media is one task. Evaluating how readers take mental shortcuts when absorbing it all is very much another.

Rules of Thumb: Anchors Ahoy!

A related rule of thumb is **primacy**. This is the way people attach most importance to the first information they come across. They see it as automatically more substantive than information they encounter later on. Another term for this is **anchoring**. Anchoring studies show how hard it is to dispel rumours or to correct misinformation. We tend to weight information not on its merits, but on the basis of *when* we get it. New information is interpreted in relation to whatever we've heard before, and sometimes *mis*interpreted as a result.

In a classic demonstration of anchoring, researchers asked groups of students to estimate what age Mahatma Gandhi was when he died. The correct answer is 78. By way of assistance, they told some of the students that the answer was 'older than 64,' while they told other students that the correct age was 'older than 9.' The average guesses provided by the two groups of students turned out to be, respectively, 99.6 and 50.1. In other words, students given the lower 'anchor' ended up providing much lower guesses. This was the case even though the 'anchor' number they were given—9—was so unhelpful as to be completely irrelevant (Strack & Mussweiler, 1997).

This is what is most powerful about anchoring. Even information we believe to be *irrelevant* can end up influencing our conclusions, by shifting our frame of reference towards an anchor.

A frequently encountered everyday example is when a vendor places a high asking price on something they want to sell. That price then becomes the focal point— the anchor—for subsequent discussion. The opening gambit in any negotiation will usually seek to anchor proceedings in this way. This is why experienced negotiators always put their offer on the table first.

No consideration of the psychology of Brexit would be complete without reference to a notorious example of anchoring that appeared emblazoned on the side of a now legendary red campaign bus, which drove around Britain prior to the referendum urging people to vote Leave. Famously, the wording on the bus was as follows:

> We send the EU £350 million a week.
> Let's fund our NHS instead.
> Vote Leave.
> Let's take back control.

The £350 million figure excited all sorts of attention. However, it was soon shown to be exaggerated. It was calculated in such a way as to greatly inflate the true net weekly cost of Britain's EU membership (Lichfield, 2017). It did not account for the United Kingdom rebate, inward investment in UK infrastructure by the European Union, grants and agricultural subsidies received, and so on.

Such was its unreliability, the head of the UK Statistics Authority wrote formally to then Foreign Secretary Boris Johnson to complain that plastering it onto the side of a campaign bus constituted 'a clear misuse of official statistics' (Kentish, 2017).

But it was too late. The Leave campaign had succeeded in anchoring public perceptions to their advantage. They set the tone on the issue. They stigmatised UK expenditure in a way that made people completely discount the trading advantages that their country receives in return for EU membership. They focused people's minds on bills, rather than on the fringe benefits of peace and stability in Europe. Any argument that it might in fact be reasonable for the world's richest countries to subsidise their poorer neighbours was rendered altogether moot.

All that mattered was that £350 million—per week!—was an awful lot of money. Even if the figure was allegedly meaningless.

Although the £350 million claim was widely criticised, its appearance had lasting effects. Two years after the referendum, researchers at King's College London found that 42% of voters still believe that Britain sends £350 million per week to the European Union (Carroll, 2018). The anchor continues to pull at public perceptions. When people try to imagine the costs of EU membership, their frame of reference is not guided by the latest exchequer balance sheets or the analyses of academic economists. It is shifted toward a number that was printed on the side of a bus.

To most people, a bill for £350 million is a comprehensible concept. It is much easier to visualise than many of the things economists usually talk about. It makes more sense than gross domestic product, fiscal consolidation, or the cyclically adjusted balance. Even the fact that the bus was red probably helped, by producing vivid images for the television news. The whole affair was very easy for most ordinary people to call to mind.

Given the availability heuristic, such memorability no doubt helped to perpetuate the bus's message. Technical footnotes about statistical particulars simply blended into background noise.

Many studies have shown that correcting misinformation frequently fails to change people's minds, especially when they have committed themselves to a particular political view (Nyhan & Reifler, 2010). If you tell people what they want to hear, they will hear it. And if you plaster it onto the side of a bus, that will do the job just as nicely.

Rules of Thumb: Give It to Me Exactly…

Sometimes instead of exaggerating, campaigners find a way to make information simply *sound* more significant than it really is. Typically this is done by going into detail, even when details are unnecessary. This approach is referred to as **implied precision**, or, more damningly, **illusory accuracy**.

In reality, specifically phrased statements are always less logically defensible than vague ones. This is because they contain more separate assertions, all of which must be true at the same time in order for the statement overall to be true. As we saw in Chapter 1 when discussing parsimony, more points of detail mean more points of weakness.

Consider the following two statements:

- Vague: 'The pound has fallen in value since Brexit'
- Specific: 'The pound has fallen in value *because of* Brexit'.

Technically, the specific version contains two assertions rather than one. These are: (a) that the pound has fallen in value since Brexit; and (b) that Brexit caused this fall. All other things being equal, the chances of two things happening at once are more remote than the chances of either thing happening on its own. A *coincidence* is always less likely than a single *incident* (Hughes, 2016). Therefore, unless there is strong supporting evidence, a specific claim should always be treated as harder to believe than a vague one.

The problem is that most people consider the opposite to be true. They find specific claims *more* persuasive than vague ones. People are susceptible to what is called the **conjunction fallacy** (Tversky & Kahneman, 1982). They falsely believe that the conjunction of two points is more probable than one point on its own. They are persuaded by the implied precision of the more specific statement.

Implied precision presents particular risks when information is expressed as numbers. It is often reasonable to summarise a figure using language such as 'around 17 million.' This factors in a loose margin of error, and in so doing, protects the overall accuracy of the information. However, it sounds more convincing when you say '17.4 million,' because that version contains more information. Most people react to numerical precision by attaching greater significance to information, even if the additional precision is of little real consequence (Johnson & Gluck, 2016).

In this way, when describing the number of voters who voted for Brexit, referring to '17.4 million' is more impressive than referring to 'around 17 million.' Numerical precision is another powerful rhetorical tool that capitalises on the rules of thumb people use when taking mental shortcuts through everyday decisions.

Rules of Thumb: What's Mine Is, Well, Mine

Much political discourse seeks to capitalise on a rule of thumb known as the **endowment effect**. This is where you overvalue something simply because you own it, and are overly threatened when someone wants to take it away. People generally attach greater value to things they possess now, compared to the amount of money they would spend to acquire the same things new (Pryor, Perfors, & Howe, 2018).

Economists discuss this concept by comparing 'willingness to pay' (the amount of money you would pay in order to buy something) with 'willingness to accept' (the amount of money you would accept from someone to purchase that same thing from you). The endowment effect is the tendency for a person's 'willingness to pay' for something to be lower than the amount they would be 'willingness to accept' to give it up should they own it.

To put it all more simply: have you ever felt so attached to a possession that you were reluctant to swap it for something else of equivalent (or even greater) monetary value? Do you remember that sense of attachment to the possession you suddenly wanted to keep? That sentimental feeling? That feeling is the endowment effect.

Talented politicians are adept at trading on people's susceptibility to the endowment effect. They subtly seek to emphasise people's ownership of things. Ownership and property are frequently invoked as rhetorical devices when campaigners argue for or against Brexit: 'your' country is under threat from the European Union; 'your' rights as an EU citizen are being taken away.

The infamous red bus contained two striking examples. Its call to action was: '*Let's fund our NHS instead.*' Referring to it as 'our' NHS was intended to make people value the NHS more, and thereby heighten concern about its finances. The slogan '*Let's take back control*' was another appeal to the endowment effect. It not only emphasised ownership (of control), but had the added oomph of invoking a threat of theft.

The endowment effect ensures we are disproportionately reluctant to give up something that we feel we own. As such, a message that something is being stolen from us will always be extremely impactful (Pettifor, 2016).

Being able to capitalise on psychological rules of thumb does not make a political campaign unscrupulous. It is not unreasonable for citizens to be reminded that they own the NHS. In many cases these tactics are a sign of exemplary political communication. They show that the campaigners have an insightful understanding of their audience.

When political campaigners take advantage of the things like the availability heuristic, anchoring, implied precision, or the endowment effect, they are not being dishonest or coercive. They are being good at political campaigning.

Consider the slogans used by groups during the Brexit referendum itself. There were three major campaign groups on the Remain side. These were their slogans:

- '*Stronger, Safer, Better Off*' (Britain Stronger in Europe)
- '*Labour In for Britain*' (Labour Party)
- '*Yes to Europe*' (Green Party).

On the Leave side, there were two major groups, which ran with the following:

- '*Let's Take Back Control*' (Vote Leave)
- '*We Want Our Country Back*' (United Kingdom Independence Party).

Even an initial glance shows the difference in style between the two sides. The Remain slogans varied in style and content. One of them offered three reasons for continued EU membership (strength, safety, and affluence), while the other two offered none.

Listing three benefits might seem to add heft, but it also creates complexity. Readers have to absorb and interpret three separate concepts. In terms of what psychologists refer to as processing time, such a slogan strains the audience's attention-span.

The Labour and Green slogans took the form of an **appeal to authority**. The Labour message was that voters should do what the Labour Party was doing. The Green Party slogan emphasised Europe rather than the Greens themselves, but still did not offer a reason for voting Remain other than the fact that they wanted you to do so. An appeal to authority is a recognised method of persuasion, but it is entirely rhetorical and therefore weak. In philosophical terms, it has no empirical or rational force.

By contrast, both Leave slogans emphasised a similar message. Both invoked the endowment effect. The two slogans appealed directly to voters' sense of ownership of Britain, arguing that this ownership was threatened. Without needing to provide a reasoned case or any empirical evidence (these were, after all, just slogans), the campaigners were able to anchor the agenda to this question of *who owns 'our' country?* Doing so bypassed the debate on whether countries should pool their sovereignty on certain matters, imposing the assumption that they should not.

In summary, the two Leave slogans were sharply focused, accurately targeted at voters' concerns, and emotionally forceful.

Political communication is an inexact science. However, on the basis that some efforts at communication are more effective than others, we can begin to quantify matters in a rudimentary way. We can say that the Leave messages were more consistent than the Remain ones, and that they made better (or, at least, more discernible) use of what is known about the psychology of decision-making. They showed a deeper understanding of the national audience and a more authentic appreciation of voters' concerns.

The Leave campaign outperformed their Remain counterparts in several critical respects. They were more successful in engaging with voters on a sentimental level. They were correctly tuned to the intuitive wavelength of their target audience. Their messages landed far more effectively, time after time.

Compared to their Remainer counterparts, the Leave campaign enjoyed a significant debating advantage: by and large, they exhibited much higher levels of emotional intelligence.

Peer Pressure: Nothing to Lose but Your Sense of Perspective

Many of our mental shortcuts are intertwined with our social lives. Interpersonal influences determine the shape of knowledge. In a democracy, the flow of beliefs across society is a matter of particular concern. We will discuss the issue of social identity and group dynamics in detail in Chapter 3. For the moment, however, we will focus on how other people affect our decision-making.

The way we perceive ourselves and, more importantly, our *tribe*, is particularly influential. We tend to consider our own group to be diverse, while believing our opponents to be all the same. With Brexit, the most obvious tribal divide is that between Remainers and Leavers. And, it would appear, both groups do indeed consider their own side to have the more nuanced insights, to have thought more deeply about the issues, and to represent a wider range of views and beliefs. Meanwhile, both dismiss the other side for being simplistic, for clinging to clichés and tropes, and for the narrowness of their obsessions.

Psychologically, we are biased to believe that we are very interesting people. We are colourful in our individuality, with wide-ranging views, many deep ideas, and an overall detailed existence. In short, we find ourselves to be terrific company. We are extremely well rounded—exactly the type of people you would like to have, say, running the country.

By contrast, we consider our opponents to be much a less varied bunch. In fact, from our perspective, they basically seem all the same. Several studies confirm that people classify their in-group communities into far more categories than they use when describing an out-group. This distortion is known as the **out-group homogeneity effect** (Judd & Park, 1988). It is as though the psychological distance between groups equates to physical distance. From afar, the details start to look a little blurry.

It goes without saying that we consider our perceived tribal diversity to be a strength rather than a weakness. We see ourselves as open-minded, welcoming of diversity in opinion, encouraging of debate and dissent, and having a mixture of good and bad ideas. When one of our tribe does something wrong, we can point out that our black sheep are outnumbered by the white. Our diversity and range are not just a sign of merit, they offer us a shield, a way of diffusing responsibility from blame.

Correspondingly, we consider our opponent tribe's homogeneity to be a sign of its limitations. The other tribe is one-eyed, single-minded, and rigidly resistant to reason. They have mostly bad ideas. And when one of them steps out of line, it reflects on them all. It reveals the type of people that they really are.

For many Remainers, Leavers are the type of people who are closed-minded, reckless, and impatient to bend the rules (e.g. Cohen, 2018). Meanwhile, for many Leavers, Remainers are a bloc of metropolitan elites, intellectual snobs, and mushy-hearted luvvies (e.g., Letts, 2017).

Consider the autocompleted search descriptions generated by the Google search engine when you type in a suitable opening phrase. These

automatic suggestions are based on what users in general have most frequently searched for on the internet. As of June 2019, entering a search
for 'Brexiteers are' produces the following dropdown list:

Brexiteers are
brexiteers are **ignorant**
brexiteers are **fascists**
brexiteers are **liars**
brexiteers are **evil**
brexiteers are **traitors**
brexiteers are **thick**
brexiteers are **deluded**
brexiteers are **angry**.

We can safely assume that these expressions are not being used by Brexiteers
to conduct searches about themselves.

Meanwhile, typing 'Remainers are' into the search box gives us these:

Remainers are
remainers are **traitors**
remainers are **cowards**
remainers are **arrogant**
remainers are **ignorant**
remainers are **middle class**
remainers are **thick**
remainers are **fascists**
remainers are **deluded**
remainers are **scum**
remainers are **more intelligent**.

Okay, maybe that last one *was* by Remainers themselves.

Out-group homogeneity is clearly an impediment to conflict resolution.
If anything, it is an ingredient in the most sinister inter-group conflicts.
The history of humanity has been punctuated by gruesome episodes where
out-groups have been tarred with a single brush. Wars have been fought on

the belief that enemy tribes were one-dimensional, rigidly alien, and universally culpable for bad actors. At the very least, out-group homogeneity impedes the seriousness of inter-group engagement. Why even bother to reach out to a narrower and less reasoned sect?

Out-group homogeneity is a powerful mental shortcut that encourages in-group loyalty. This is all very well, so long as yours is the only group that matters. But of course it is never the case (and never should be) that only one group matters.

This problem relates to the mental shortcut called **splitting**, sometimes referred to as **bifurcation** or **binary thinking**. Essentially, splitting is the habit of dichotomising all things into two categories, the absolutely 'good' and the absolutely 'bad'. The habit is often seen in infants, for whom life is brutally simplified, consisting of either positive feelings (being warm, fed, looked after, and stimulated) or negative ones (being cold, hungry, lonely, or neglected). For many psychologists, this infant habit of splitting remains at the backs of our minds even as we grow into adults. We resurrect it when we are under stress or otherwise finding it difficult to cope with the adult world. At a societal level, it accentuates all political divides (Richards, 2019).

Not every psychologist links splitting to childhood experiences. Many believe we are prone to binary thinking for the simple reason that it helps us to make decisions more quickly. Whatever its origins, there is no doubt as to its power. Most people are overly prone to 'either-or' or 'them-and-us' thinking.

These habits help to explain why group polarisation occurs, as it has with Brexit. Prior to the 2016 referendum, Eurobarometer survey data suggested that British people held a wide range of opinions about the European Union, creating several distinct subgroups in the population. However, that was when the European Union was a lower-tier political issue. After the referendum, things changed dramatically. Now there are essentially two groups. Stress has happened, and so splitting has occurred. We will return to the problem of group polarisation in Chapter 3.

A sure sign of splitting is when two groups end up seeing two different realities. In partisan politics, observers are often exasperated at the way their adversaries reject what appear to them to be facts.

'Facts are facts!' is a frequent plaintive cry (which, in Brexit, is often uttered by people who complain about 'Leave means Leave' being a tautology). In reality, our mental shortcuts make us quite capable of playing very fast and very loose with facts. Everybody does so, to some extent.

Peer Pressure: Truthiness

We are all surprisingly comfortable with what psychologists call **illusory truth** (Begg, Anas, & Farinacci, 1992). This is where an assertion becomes believed simply because it is stated and stated repeatedly. It is a principle of psycholinguistics—the psychology of language—that people can derive meaning from grammar as well as from substance. In effect, substance is optional.

In the 1950s, Noam Chomsky gave the following example of a semantically meaningless sentence (Chomsky, 1957):

- '*Colourless green ideas sleep furiously*'.

Chomsky, for once, was not talking about politics. Instead his point was to explain the distinction between syntax and semantics. A sentence can be syntactically correct while being semantically nonsensical. However, the way our brains navigate language means that, when we hear such a sentence, the very fact it is grammatically intact strikes us as making it valid. Our gut reaction is that there must be some meaning in there somewhere. We believe that the sentence *sounds* meaningful. So our brains—those pattern-detecting engines—start working to figure out what that meaning must be.

The danger is that, when we fail to figure out the meaning, we persist in our belief that the statement must be meaningful. This is because we are biased to assume that information presented to us is valid. It is one of our standard '**conversational conventions**', our rules of thumb for navigating human dialogue (Holbrook, Krosnick, Carson, & Mitchell, 2000).

We are especially prone to doing so when the statement is repeated over and over. When we see other people accepting the statement, we assume that *they* must know what it means, making us even more inclined to go along with it. In reality, however, *they* are probably watching *us* nodding along, and concluding that *we* must know the true meaning. This dynamic of mutually reinforced misinformation produces what is referred to as **pluralistic ignorance** (Marsh & Yang, 2018).

Instead of colourless green ideas sleeping furiously, we might instead be presented with some of the following statements:

- *'No deal is better than a bad deal'*
- *'Let's have our cake and eat it'*
- *'We will have no checks at the border and simultaneously opt out of freedom-of-movement'*
- *'A people's vote is different to a second referendum'.*

Each of these statements is at best vague and at worst self-contradictory. However, their repetition is powerful. It fosters a feeling of meaningfulness. Their grammatical soundness conveys a form of validity. Several studies have shown that information is more likely to be rated as true the more often it is repeated (Polage, 2012). When it comes to political sloganeering, familiarity trumps rationality.

There are grounds to suspect that false political beliefs are especially hard to shift. Researchers at Cambridge University have concluded that prevention would be much better than cure. They have started work to develop a fake news 'vaccine', a way of inoculating the public against the spread of misinformation (van der Linden, Leiserowitz, Rosenthal, & Maibach, 2017). Their focus will be on designing messages to warn people that bad information is coming, as well as arming them with pre-emptive refutations. The vaccine itself takes the form of a small dose of fake news, which people can practice their refutations on. This is supposed to help them 'build up resistance' to misinformation, by providing a 'repertoire' of critical thinking skills (BBC News, 2017). You would be forgiven for thinking this type of thing has been attempted before.

In the meantime, the results of illusory truths will continue to be felt. Psychologists who study the **backfire effect** have shown that presenting people with disconfirming evidence often does little to change their minds. In many cases, it has the opposite paradoxical effect of making them more committed than ever to their original view (Flynn, Nyhan, & Reifler, 2017).

With Brexit, it sometimes feels as though the more people are bombarded with opposing arguments, the more rigidly they stick to their own starting positions. People engage in **identity-protective motivated reasoning** such that counter-arguments only serve to exacerbate existing divisions (Kahan, Jenkins-Smith, & Braman, 2011). The role of social identity on shaping people's behaviour is important, and we will discuss this in more detail in Chapter 3.

It is notable that despite constant public attention given to Brexit since 2016, the vast majority of voters have simply stuck to their initial views. Nearly three years after the referendum, opinion polls suggest that 90% of both Leavers and Remainers have just not changed their minds (Curtice, 2019). The endless political discussion, the radio phone-ins, the marches on the streets, as well as general, local, and European elections, all appear to have had little effects on people's attitudes—except, perhaps, to harden them.

With Brexit we often seem to have entered a downward spiral. The more that 'experts' present reasons as to why Brexit is a bad idea, the more committed some people become to seeing Brexit through to the end. A key force here is that of power, both real and perceived. In many senses, Brexit is propelled by an assertion of personal power, a desire to make choices irrespective of what others have to say. We will return to this dynamic of power, choice, and backlash in Chapter 3.

Problems of Rose-Tinted Glasses: Everything Is Awesome

The final selection of mental shortcuts is, in some senses, the most stereotypically human. It is the quaint but incorrigible tendency people have to consider themselves, and their own kind, as awesome.

A famous example is the **Dunning-Kruger effect**, where people mistakenly overestimate their own abilities, often in the face of conspicuous evidence of personal weakness. They willingly volunteer to serve at a level far beyond that at which they can adequately perform. They have a belief that they are capable when in fact they are not.

This self-perceived capability has been memorably called 'the miscalibration of the incompetent' (Kruger & Dunning, 1999). However, that description involves some unfair victim-blaming. The point here is that, as humans, we are *all* incompetent at some things. Some of us are incompetent at many things.

The problem is that we naturally recognise what we *can* do, but relatively fail to recognise what we *can't*. Sooner or later, we all fall victim to the Dunning-Kruger effect. The very nature of the effect is that we are oblivious to it when it happens.

Human beings are terrible at judging their own competence. You could say that they are incompetent at it. Time after time, people put themselves forward with great aplomb for jobs that they are egregiously ill-prepared to carry out.

This can lead to a Secretary of State for Exiting the EU declaring that he 'hadn't quite understood' the importance of cross-Channel trade to the UK economy (Merrick, 2018), or a Shadow Home Secretary being unsure whether her proposed police recruitment plan would cost £300,000 or maybe £8 million (Gillett, 2017), and a Northern Ireland Secretary who was not aware of the basic structure of the Northern Irish political conflict when she agreed to take on the job (Embury-Dennis, 2018).

Even the ablest people can eventually overreach to such an extent that it becomes unclear that they understand their own limitations.

This problem is perpetuated by **confirmation bias**, the habit of focusing on whatever supports your own perception, while overlooking whatever might threaten it. In Chapter 1, we saw how people who argue that Brexit is linked to the fall of empire are often guilty of confirmation bias. They discuss confirmatory examples, but not contradictory cases. They argue that post-imperial nationalistic fervour puts British people off the EU, without explaining why it does not have the same effect on people in other post-imperial countries.

Confirmation bias is ever-present in the Brexit saga (ironically, it is easy to think of ways in which this assertion is true). Leave campaigners focus on positive opportunities for trade, but overlook the technical challenges of tariffs. Remain campaigners focus on the prospect of pan-national harmony, but overlook the shortcomings of a European Parliament that institutionally eschews a formal government–opposition dynamic, thereby marginalising dissent.

Such reasoning makes logic incomplete. The more scientific approach would be to focus not on confirmatory evidence, but on factors that might falsify your presumptions. Scientists are often accused of being know-it-alls. In reality, scientists operate on the basis that everything they *think* they know might be wrong. Science relies on a systematic effort to disprove things. Real scientists don't look for proof, they look for disproof.

The presence of even a single counterexample raises doubt over any theory. Confirmation bias is the habit of failing to apply this important test. It reflects unwarranted faith in our own judgements. We view our opinions through rose-tinted glasses.

Most of us have the habit of deflecting blame while inviting praise. We are prone to a mental shortcut known as **causal attribution bias** (Stiensmeier-Pelster & Heckhausen, 2018). When events go against us, we blame outside forces that lie beyond our control. But when events turn out well, we proclaim our own input and influence.

A student who does poorly on an examination will bemoan the difficulty of the exam questions, whereas one who does well will take pride in their ability to study (and, perhaps, their innate intelligence). A player who loses a game will question the referee's performance, while one who wins will shake the referee's hand and accept their plaudits. All of us are prone to this type of distorted, self-serving reasoning.

Attribution bias encourages people to take credit for success and to deflect blame for failure. It is one of the reasons voters criticise politicians even though it is they who elected them. Politicians themselves claim credit for what are often random occurrences, such as short-term upticks in the economy. Meanwhile, should the economy decline, world economic forces will be held to be responsible.

A consequence of this uneven distribution of credit and blame is that people often persist with faulty strategies, even when they are failing rapidly.

Nine days before the date originally planned for Britain to leave the European Union, Prime Minister Theresa May stepped into an oak-panelled room in 10 Downing Street and stood before the waiting television cameras. The media had been summoned at short notice, told only that the Prime Minister would deliver a speech. Tantalisingly, television networks were advised that they should interrupt their normal schedules. What the Prime Minister was about to say would warrant live national broadcast.

Earlier that afternoon, she had been informed by EU Council president Donald Tusk that Britain could only extend the Article 50 process if its parliament approved her withdrawal deal. However, the speaker of the House of Commons had ruled that with her deal already having been defeated twice, the Prime Minister would not be allowed to put it forward a third time. As such, Tusk's condition could not be met. The Prime Minister was out of options.

When members of the press were informed of arrangements for an impromptu night-time televised speech, many of them concluded that the Prime Minister was about to call a general election. Some of them thought she would resign. She did neither of things.

Instead, in a stern voice and with eyes to camera, the Prime Minister went into full-blown attribution mode:

> In March 2017, I triggered the Article 50 process for the UK to exit the EU
> – and Parliament supported it overwhelmingly. Two years on, MPs have
> been unable to agree on a way to implement the UK's withdrawal. As a
> result, we will now not leave on time with a deal on 29 March.

Her words claimed personal credit for initiating the withdrawal process. But when it came to explaining its failures, the Prime Minister lambasted MPs for failing to approve her deal. The delay in Brexit was 'a result' of *their* behaviour, she said, not hers. She continued:

> And of this I am absolutely sure: you the public have had enough. You are
> tired of the infighting. You are tired of the political games and the arcane
> procedural rows. Tired of MPs talking about nothing else but Brexit when
> you have real concerns…So far, Parliament has done everything possible to

avoid making a choice. Motion after motion and amendment after amendment have been tabled without Parliament ever deciding what it wants. All MPs have been willing to say is what they do not want.

Again her message was simple. She had succeeded, by triggering Article 50. Others—namely, MPs—had failed, by rejecting the deal she had negotiated.

She made no allowance that perhaps others too were responsible for initiating the withdrawal process, or that she too was partly responsible for its delay. After all, it was the product of *her* negotiation that MPs were refusing to approve. Not only that, she had created her own jeopardy by assuring the EU that Parliament would indeed pass her deal. In fact, they rejected it overwhelmingly. The deal went down to the heaviest parliamentary defeat ever seen in the democratic era (Stewart, 2019).

The Prime Minister's self-justifying words were greeted, literally, with gasps. The assembled television microphones picked up an exasperated off-camera voice replying 'Oh please!' as the Prime Minister left the lectern (Davidson, 2019). One major newspaper described it as 'the single worst speech she has ever given' (Peck, 2019). The very fact that the Prime Minister's speech was unanimously condemned reflected just how powerfully the attribution effect had skewed her perspective.

Problems of Rose-Tinted Glasses: Everything Is Under Control

Many studies have shown that people are biased toward a kind of generalised, but unreasonable, optimism. They consider themselves to be highly able, destined for success, and in control of situations.

This bias is useful for promoting persistence, and is mentally healthy. In fact, it can be considered a *sign* of good mental health. Research suggests that people with *poor* mental health are much less likely to display this kind of bias, instead exhibiting what is referred to as **depressive realism** (Feltham, 2016). Our **illusions of control** keep us going in life. They assist us to stave off depression by emboldening us in the face of risk (Taylor & Brown, 1988).

As evolved beings, our brains are primed to over-estimate our chances of success in a given challenge. It has long been observed that gamblers will bet more money on the roll of a dice if they are allowed to touch the dice themselves instead of having a croupier roll it for them (Langer, 1975). Brexit is that lottery ticket we promised ourselves would be the final one, the winnings from which we expect will provide a justifying return on our investment.

We attach unrealistically high value to events that we have made happen ourselves, regardless of the quality of the results. This disproportionate pride in our own handiwork has been called the **IKEA effect** (Norton, Mochon, & Ariely, 2012). Brexit is that slightly wonky credenza prominently adorning our front hallway, the target of awkwardly forced praise from polite but discomfited visitors.

After we have committed to a decision, we are inclined to stick to it. When we purchase something expensive, we bias our reasoning to conclude that it was, in fact, good value after all, a process called **post-purchase rationalisation** (Park & Hill, 2018). Brexit is that anti-wrinkle cream that we convince ourselves makes us look younger.

All this might explain why people who support Brexit are often very confident about the post-Brexit future, even though many experts disagree. Meanwhile, people who support Remain are confident that a second referendum would see their side emerge victorious, despite opinion polls suggesting that such an outcome is far from certain.

Ultimately, everyone is inclined toward the view that their preferred outcome will eventuate. Everyone feels that their influence will carry the day.

Problems of Rose-Tinted Glasses: It's Not Me, It's You

All of the mental shortcuts discussed above—the rules of thumb, the peer pressure effects, and the problems of rose-tinted glasses—sound plausible, have been demonstrated in empirical research, and are *exactly* the kinds of thing that make *other people* so infuriating. But of course, we would never fall into these pitfalls ourselves, now, would we?

Well, our final example of the problem of rose-tinted glasses is the **third-person effect**—the belief that reasoning errors, subjective biases, and social influence all affect *other* people more than they affect us (Kim, 2016). This is the true meta-bias, the bias that is perpetuated by all the other biases.

The availability heuristic helps us remember examples of our own savvy. Confirmation bias ensures that we focus on them. Because of out-group homogeneity bias, we falsely consider other people to be less adept than ourselves. An illusion of control makes us believe we are resistant to social influence. And we are oblivious of evidence to the contrary because of the Dunning-Kruger effect.

The third-person effect helps explain why Brexit attitudes are so frequently pathologised. Both Remainers and Leavers decry the other side for being gullible, unreasonable, and misled. Meanwhile they presume themselves to be immune from those very afflictions.

In reality, we are all subject to the normal standards of human reasoning. We all use rules of thumb, we are all swayed by social influence, and we all view ourselves through rose-tinted glasses. The overarching error is to falsely assume for ourselves—or for others—a kind of robotic rationality that isn't really there.

Appreciating the role of habitual mental shortcuts may help us understand how people reason through Brexit. It may even provide a means to escape the quagmire.

People and Their Feelings

In a democracy, you might expect that voters will go to great lengths to fulfil their duties with care. Psychologists have long pointed out that people are much more expedient than that.

Far from investigating the issues that affect a referendum or an election, it often makes more sense to remain ignorant. Given that yours is a single vote, among, literally, tens of millions of others, it is most unlikely that the paper *you* place into the ballot box will ever be decisive. No doubt this will sound sacrilegious in some quarters—but in that sense, *your democratic vote doesn't really matter.*

Your personal franchise is irrelevant in the greater scheme of things. As such, if you go to extreme lengths—or any lengths at all—to research the issues on which you are voting, then you could say that was little more than a way to wantonly squander your time. Consider yourself in isolation: the cost, in time and effort, of conducting any investigations to inform yourself will always exceed the direct benefit you garner from casting your single vote. This is because the direct benefit is zero. If you simply stay at home on voting day, absolutely nothing different will happen.

Such a cold cost-benefit calculation, where it makes no sense to gather information, is called the principle of **rational ignorance** (Downs, 1957). But there's more. Not only does it make sense for you to remain ignorant, it also makes sense for you not to think too hard about any of it. You are free to decide which way to vote on a whim. You can make it up as you go along. This extension of the point has been named the principle of **rational irrationality** (Caplan, 2001). Perhaps those one-in-ten voters in the Brexit referendum were applying this principle when they turned up at polling stations not having made up their minds on whether to vote 'Leave' or 'Remain'.

Once again, it hardly matters. Your vote is infinitesimally meaningful. In other words, it is meaning*less*. It changes nothing. *Nobody cares what you think.*

It perhaps says something about the psychology of decision-making that political choice can be cogently explained using the term 'rational irrationality.'

But there you go.

One of the key psychological lessons from Brexit is to bring attention to the parlous fluidity of human reasoning. Especially, we should bear in mind that people are greatly influenced by what they perceive to be their immediate future prospects relative to their current situation. The less they have to lose, the less they fear risk. We should also remember that all people are prone to dividing the world into 'us', who are good, and 'them' who are bad, and to fail to appreciate the cluttered rationality in our opponents.

The fact we see our adversaries as uncompromising, unreceptive, and unreachable distracts from the reality that we too are, in our own way, uncompromising, unreceptive, and unreachable. Taking a scientific approach to our personal psychologies, we should seek to falsify our own assumptions. We should interrogate our perceptions of the people we are against.

Ultimately, psychology is the scientific study of the human experience, the plight of individuals, their feelings, and their interactions with others. Human beings comprise a single species with common traits and procliv-ities. But they also vary as individuals, in temperament, inclination, and taste. They don't just think. They emote. And they treat each other—and affect each other—in different ways. We will now turn to this aspect of the psychology of Brexit: the psychology of the individual, and of the groups to which they belong.

3

The Brexit People

I. One Size Does Not Fit All

In August 2016, with Britain still reeling from the Brexit referendum, virtuoso Leave campaigner and outgoing UKIP leader Nigel Farage appeared on the Russian-owned television station, RT. He was being interviewed for *News Thing*, RT's satirical commentary show. Questions covered such topics as recycling, homophobia, animal cruelty, and, of course, the B-word. Everywhere that Nigel went, the B-word was sure to go.

At one point the interviewer challenged Farage as to whether he felt responsible for promoting an 'atmosphere of hostility' towards immigrants in Britain during the referendum campaign. Farage responded by claiming to have done the opposite.

'Quite the reverse,' he said. 'I'm not against anybody.' In fact, Farage claimed to have 'single-handedly destroyed the far right in British politics.' He argued that he did this by leading UKIP to electorally supplant the British National Party (Horton, 2016).

Farage is widely seen as a divisive figure, and the RT network itself is a controversial platform. This combination of circumstances certainly caught the eye. However, media attention for Farage's performance did

© The Author(s) 2019
B. M. Hughes, *The Psychology of Brexit*,
https://doi.org/10.1007/978-3-030-29364-2_3

not focus on his claims or political arguments. Instead, all the buzz was about something else: Nigel's facial hair.

Yes, heretofore a clean-shaven stockbroker forever garbed in either pinstripe suits or landed-gentry tweed, Farage was now, conspicuously, sporting a new fashion statement. Here it was. A moustache. It was all anyone could see.

A '70s porntache,' the *Guardian* called it, 'face fuzz…a two headed droopy caterpillar' (Elan, 2016).

Unsurprisingly, social media also weighed in: 'retired major at the golf club'; 'the most preposterous moustache in British politics'; 'like a villain from an old detective movie'; 'a Victorian melodrama'; 'Will Ferrell from Anchorman'; 'Manuel from Fawlty Towers'; 'up there with the worse things ever to exist on this planet'; and—perhaps most damningly—'worse than Brexit' (Cooper, 2016; Duell, 2016; Horton, 2016; Payne, 2016).

'You know when Farage said he was resigning so that he could be himself?' somebody on Twitter asked, 'Did he literally mean he just wanted to grow a moustache?'

Facial hair is always going to attract attention. Sometimes it will be negative. Shortly afterwards, the Farage tache vanished, never to be seen again.

Which is perhaps just as well. After all, according to opinion pollsters, facial hair is more of a 'Remain' thing. In November 2016, YouGov conducted a detailed large-scale national survey on precisely this matter. They found that 53% of Leave-voting British women report a preference for clean-shaven men, compared to just 40% of women who voted Remain (Smith, 2017a).

Leaver women were found to show a slight preference for their menfolk to sport visible chest hair, suggesting that it is not hair per se that causes them a problem. Just hair on men's faces.

And there's more.

YouGov have also established that Leavers are twice as likely as Remainers to prefer their steaks well done. However, they are just half as likely to eat their steaks with gravy (Belam, 2017). London-based Leave voters have a better understanding of cockney-rhyming slang than their Remain-voting neighbours (Smith, 2017b). And while Leavers believe that Doctor Who would be more likely to vote Conservative than Labour in a general election, Remainers believe the Gallifreyan Time Lord would vote Labour rather than Conservative (Smith, 2017c).

Moustaches, rhyming slang, steak with gravy, and the voting intentions of fictional time travellers are not the only things that divide Leavers from Remainers. Political issues come up too. While more than a quarter of Leave voters say they would like the UK to emulate the United States in withdrawing from the Paris climate change agreement, only five per cent of Remain voters would support such an action (Rogers & Ostfeld, 2017).

And there is, let us not forget, that whole issue regarding the European Union.

The very fact there was a referendum for Brexit leads many people to think of EU membership as a point of political divide. But there are many other intriguing differences between Remainers and Leavers. They are distinctive in their tastes, their perceptions of British culture, and their attitudes to things like climate change.

Brexit is far more than just political. It reflects how British citizens psychologically experience their lives, how they identify themselves culturally, and what values they hold. Trying to sort out Brexit by focusing on global trade, regulatory alignment, or confirmatory referendums risks missing the most important point of all.

The resolution of Brexit needs to account for people's personalities, their emotions, and their sense of place in the world.

Brexit is psychological, not political.

Know Your Audience

Psychologists talk a lot about what people 'in general' are like, what people 'in general' do, and how people 'in general' feel. However, at its core, psychology is not the study of people in general. It is the study of people as individuals.

You see, not everybody is the same. People vary. When we say that people 'in general' are like this, do that, or feel the other, we mean it as a summary. We are talking about tendencies that we observe in many human beings, perhaps even most of them, but never them all. One of the great insights of psychology has been to reveal the incredible variability that characterises the human condition.

We are not, as individuals, truly unique. Patterns do arise and many of our behaviours are predictable. However, the range of human thoughts, feelings, and behaviours, while finite and distinctly human, is also vast. Humankind is characterised by its diversity. One size does not fit all.

For that reason, it is always dangerous to generalise, to assume that how one person is reflects how other people are. It is dangerous to try to summarise an entire group of people using a single point of description.

For example, the cliché that 'men are from Mars while women are from Venus' overlooks the fact that many men are quite like many women and many women resemble many men. Most beliefs about gender differences in psychology—such as the idea that men have better mathematical ability than women—are simply sexist stereotypes (Hyde, 2014). They owe their existence to mental shortcuts, such as how the availability heuristic drives us to remember eye-catching, but non-representative, examples. In reality, both men and women are from the same place: Earth (Carothers & Reis, 2013).

The dangers of over-simplification are sometimes linked to what social scientists call the 'ecological fallacy' (Russo, 2017). This term refers to a mistake that many people make when interpreting statistical data: they draw conclusions about individuals in a group when all they have to go on is group-level information.

If you know that a person comes from a neighbourhood with a high crime rate, you are committing the ecological fallacy if you presume that person to have criminal tendencies. If you know that English men are, on average, 1.34 cm taller than English women (Moody, 2013), then you are committing the ecological fallacy if you presume that Raheem Sterling is taller than Theresa May (he isn't).

Likewise, if you know that the majority of people in the United Kingdom voted Leave in the Brexit referendum, it does not allow you to state baldly that the will of the British people is to withdraw from the European Union.

This phrase—'the will of the British people'—has proven controversial precisely because of this point. There is no single will. People vary. Referring simply to the will of the people, and making key decisions on that basis, is an example of the ecological fallacy. One size does not fit all. The best that can be described is the will of the *majority* of the British people, which, of course, is a very different thing.

It is also a very tentative thing. As we saw in Chapter 2, people who voted for Brexit defined the idea in many different ways. Therefore, even among the majority who voted Leave, there is no single 'will.'

This is not merely a pedantic point of vocabulary. There are practical implications to this type of error. For example, many MPs argue that, when voting in Parliament, they need to reflect the wishes of the electors who put them there.

Of the 650 MPs in the House of Commons, more than 400 are Remainers whose constituencies returned Leave majorities in the Brexit referendum (Hughes, 2017). After the referendum, a majority of these MPs announced that they would switch their position to support the Brexit process. Many now refer to themselves as Leavers. Their argument is often that 'the people who elected them' voted Leave, so their duty as MPs is to respect this.

However, it is wrong to interpret a pro-Brexit majority at constituency-level with a pro-Brexit majority *among the particular voters who vote for the local MP.*

One example is the constituency of Don Valley in South Yorkshire. In the Brexit referendum, Don Valley had one of the highest Leave votes in the country. Around 68% of its voters supported Leave (Hanretty, 2017). The sitting Labour MP campaigned for Remain, but then changed her position after the result was known. She has since supported Brexit very stridently. As she explains, 'I promised my voters that I would accept the referendum' (Flint, 2019).

The referendum turnout was 60%, which means that the 68% Leave vote in Don Valley equated to 41% of the constituency's voters. In other words, just a minority of the constituents are on record as having supporting Brexit.

Prior to the referendum, the MP for Don Valley was elected to Parliament on 46% of votes from a 60% turnout. This means that the people this MP refers to as 'her voters' comprised just 28% of her constituents.

It is therefore quite parlous to presume that Don Valley's Brexit voters were necessarily the same people who elected the constituency's MP, or that the voters who chose the MP went on to support Brexit (Ford, 2018). If anything, there are grounds to suspect that Labour voters in places like Don Valley are, in fact, mostly Remainers (Crerar, 2018).

Constituency MPs will consider many factors when deciding whether to change their public positions on the major political issues of the day. However, in general, it would be incorrect for an MP to conclude that 'her voters' support Brexit simply on the basis that this was the aggregate referendum vote in her constituency.

Making such an inference over-generalises a single summary point (the local referendum result) and so is an example of the ecological fallacy.

As it happens, just 34 MPs found themselves in the opposite position to the MP in Don Valley. Their constituencies voted Remain, but they support Leave (Sandhu, 2018). In fact, many of them are leading pro-Brexit voices in British politics. These MPs stuck to their Leave positions after the referendum, and virtually all were successfully re-elected in the 2017 general election. Their Remain-voting constituents clearly did not form the majority of voters who elect them, suggesting that these MPs may have had a better grasp of the ecological fallacy.

Personality Goes a Long Way

In the Quentin Tarantino movie *Pulp Fiction*, there is a lengthy section of dialogue in which two characters debate why it is acceptable for humans to eat pigs but not dogs. It revolves around the belief that dogs have 'better personalities.' The implication is that if a pig had a better personality, it would cease to be a filthy animal. Both characters agree. 'Personality,' one of them remarks, 'goes a long way' (Yamamoto, 1999).

But when we talk about personality in psychology, we rarely talk about 'better' or 'worse'. Most scientific research in psychology views human personalities as comprising *traits*, broad character attributes that range from one extreme to another. Away from the very extremes, traits are never good or bad.

A familiar example is introversion–extraversion. A human being can be very introverted, very extraverted, or somewhere in between, but the spectrum itself is neither 'good' nor 'bad'.

Over the past century, and based on millions of survey data-points, psychologists have developed targeted questionnaires for measuring personality traits. These scales seem to work quite well. When a psychologist scores a client for introversion-extraversion, the client's friends, family, and everyone who knows them will all agree that the score makes a lot of sense. In technical language, this type of feedback is said to make the questionnaire 'valid'. It is the basis on which scientific personality assessment is designed and quality-controlled.

There is a wide scientific consensus that, while human beings have may different personality characteristics, there are five major traits on which all people can be scored. Introversion–extraversion is one: every human being will have a score somewhere on this trait. The other four are: agreeableness––hostility; emotional stability–instability (also known as 'neuroticism'); conscientiousness–unconscientiousness; and openness–caution. Of these, openness, conscientiousness, and neuroticism seem to be particularly related to people's political views (Sibley, Osborne, & Duckitt, 2012).

The process of measuring psychological traits is called 'psychometrics.' Researchers have developed psychometrics into a fine art, having identified stable patterns in huge statistical datasets compiled over decades. That said, many psychologists who ask people to fill out questionnaires seem quite unaware of their statistical basis, or the fact that some personality measures are more scientific than others (Hughes, 2018).

Questionnaires about how people like their steak are not very scientific. When we discover that Leave voters prefer their steaks well done, there is not much we can do with this information.

How a person likes their steak—or, more importantly, what they choose to say about it to opinion pollsters—is determined by many factors. It says a lot about their cultural background, such as what part of the country they come from and what socioeconomic group they are in. That can be interesting information to ponder, but it reveals relatively little about people's deep-seated psychological impulses.

Therefore, when considering research into the personality traits of Leavers and Remainers, it is important to focus on studies that use validated psychometric questionnaires. It is also important to look for other scientific strengths, such as whether the researchers have access to large representative samples of ordinary people.

One major study commissioned by the Online Privacy Foundation certainly meets these requirements. Conducted by a group of British and American social scientists, the OPF study employed the best psychometric questionnaires available, and included a sample of well over 11,000 voters (Sumner, Scofield, Buchanan, Evans, & Shearing, 2018).

The OPF found that Leave voters were slightly more extraverted than Remainers, and had slightly lower scores for openness. Statistically speaking, these two differences were very modest. In general language, you would say that they reflected small differences in personality that would probably not be noticed by many observers in the real world.

However, the main study findings were striking. Compared to Remainers, Leave voters had much higher scores for conscientiousness and much lower scores for neuroticism. In other words, Leave voters were found to be *more diligent and concerned with right-and-wrong* than Remainers, as well as *more emotionally stable*. These findings were statistically large. They were the type of personality differences that would likely be quite noticeable to most real-world observers.

The finding that Leave voters are more diligent and emotionally stable than Remain voters runs somewhat counter to the common stereotype of Eurosceptics, who are often depicted as being selfish and febrile. However, we should remember that there is no such thing as good or bad personality traits. Highly diligent people might be considered po-faced or supercilious to others. People who are very emotionally stable might come across to some as being cold or unsympathetic. In the end, personality traits do not reflect a person's moral fibre or the soundness of their judgement.

That said, the particular combination of high conscientiousness and low openness is noteworthy. This is because past research has suggested that people with this profile are more likely to report strong desires for obedience, conformity, and law and order. A number of psychologists have chosen to describe this profile as reflecting 'authoritarianism.' As such, this might imply that Leavers are relatively authoritarian.

There is now an extensive body of research that looks at authoritarianism as a personality characteristic in its own right. Therefore, the OPF research group included a separate questionnaire in their study to measure authoritarianism in detail. This confirmed that Leave-voters do indeed score higher than Remain-voters on authoritarianism questionnaires.

As such, the researchers published their finding that Leavers are more 'authoritarian' than Remainers.

This finding has been echoed in a number of other, smaller, studies. Leave voters seem more likely to hold a sense of deference towards traditional forms of authority, a desire for others to adhere to social norms, and an animosity toward circuitous thinking or unconventional behaviour.

Some researchers suggest that these characteristics are associated with a more structured style of thinking, where people prefer concrete and straightforward solutions to logic problems (Zmigrod, Rentfrow, & Robbins, 2018). Leavers want to be able to see a clear way forward. To them, the prospect of 'taking back control' is certainly appealing.

Data from the European Values Survey, which polls citizens across all EU member states, suggest that authoritarianism is a strong predictor of Euroscepticism. People who score high on authoritarianism are more likely to oppose European integration and to reject the notion of a European identity. They are also more likely to hold negative views about immigration in general, and non-local religions in particular (Tillman, 2013). Such themes echo many of those discussed in relation to Brexit.

However, we should remember that this is politics. A big problem with all such findings is terminology. 'Authoritarianism' is a very loaded term, with strongly negative connotations. What one person considers 'authoritarian', another person might see as simply 'autonomous' or, at worst, 'fastidious.'

Several questions on the OPF authoritarianism questionnaire referred to social issues like religion, traditionalism, and morality. However, Leave voters answered these questions very much in the mid-range. On an authoritarianism scale ranging from 0 to 160, younger Leavers had an average score of 73 (i.e., below the mid-point), while older Leavers had an average score of 80 (i.e., precisely on the mid-point).

So while it was technically correct to report that Leavers had higher authoritarianism than Remainers, it seems misleading to suggest that they were notably 'authoritarian'. In reality, their scores were nondescript. They were neither low nor high. They were middling. True, Remainers had lowish scores for authoritarianism. But their average score, around 50, was still closer to the mid-point than to the minimum.

The way psychologists interpret and discuss 'authoritarianism' is one of a number of terminology issues that raise serious questions about political bias in Brexit research. We will revisit this topic in detail in Chapter 5.

Another complication is the way the term 'authoritarianism' is frequently conflated with right-wing social conservatism. Indeed, one of the commonest questionnaires for measuring it is called the 'Right-Wing Authoritarianism Scale' (Altemeyer, 1998). In reality, authoritarianism cuts across the traditional right-left political divide. Voters on the left can be just as authoritarian as those on the right. While the right-left divide drove the outcome in most UK general elections up to 2017, it had little or no bearing on the outcome of the Brexit referendum. Data from the British Election Study shows that Labour-supporting Leave voters scored just as high on authoritarianism as their Conservative-supporting counterparts (Sturridge, 2018a).

The traditional left-right divide strongly reflects differences in income, wealth, and social class. By contrast, authoritarianism is more closely associated to education levels and age (Sturridge, 2018b). Recall from Chapter 2 that these very factors—education and age—were strong predictors of how people voted on Brexit.

'Authoritarian' is certainly a controversial label, and in reality Leave voters have mid-range scores for this attribute. Nonetheless, the fact that Remain voters' scores are *lower*, and therefore different, is pertinent. It means that this profile—whatever you might wish to call it—helps to shed some light on the attitudinal determinants that link age and education to Brexit.

In adding to our understanding of the psychology of Brexit, it seems indeed to be true: personality goes a long way.

Enough of Experts

At a very basic level it can be stated, without fuss or demur, that 'Brexit means Brexit.' Memorably, in July 2016, Prime Minister Theresa May made this her catchphrase. 'Brexit means Brexit,' she announced, 'and we're going to make a success of it!' She was to repeat this statement, verbatim, in many speeches over the succeeding months.

Some observers castigated the newly appointed Prime Minister for promoting a tautology as her keystone policy. However, her statement was not without rhetorical force. In declaring that 'Brexit means Brexit', she was choosing to make her point stylistically. She was saying that Brexit should not be redefined into something that is not Brexit, her implication being that there was a real and present risk such a transformation would be attempted.

It was a dig at the politics of jargon, academic obfuscation, and wonkery—where politicians try to avoid doing something difficult by doing something easy, and claiming that this is what was really intended all along. Saying that 'Brexit means Brexit' was designed to pre-emptively contradict any claim that 'Well, technically, we can do something *else*…and just *call* it "Brexit."'

Such slipperiness is common in academia, where there is a culture of rewarding people for looking at old problems in new ways. That culture is generally successful at promoting innovative creativity. However, sometimes it breeds a devilish tendency toward contrarianism, contortion of language, and obfuscation. It can bring out the worst in a certain type of intellectual, the one to beams with pride when others cannot understand them. Mind-bending logic, niche vocabulary, and allusions to esoteric background information are all customarily employed to produce an academic dialect that, by design, keeps non-specialist interlopers at arm's length.

May was striking the same chord as when Leave campaigner and then Justice Secretary Michael Gove famously declared, during the Brexit referendum campaign, that people in Britain 'have had enough of experts' (Mance, 2016). While Gove was widely vilified for this statement, it was more subtle than it first appeared.

Somewhat truncated by an interviewer interrupting his flow, Gove's sound bite was actually part of a longer, more nuanced, point (Mackey, 2016):

> I think the people of this country have had enough of experts, from organisations with acronyms, saying that they know what is best, and getting it consistently wrong. Because these people are the same ones who got consistently wrong what was happening [before the 2008 recession]…

Distrust of unquestioned experts is not in itself irrational. On the contrary, it reflects a rather scientific approach: question assertions by seeking corroboration, and give due weight to falsifying evidence. Where it unravels is when reasoned evidence-based contributions are dismissed *without* assessment. Or when distrust becomes automatic, such as when contributions are dismissed *despite* being clearly reasoned and evidence-based.

We might suspect that people described as 'authoritarian' would be inclined to trust experts, given how strongly they are supposed to value traditional symbols of authority. However, precisely who is seen as constituting an authority symbol is very much in the eye of the beholder.

Boffins who advise organisations such as the Bank of England or the International Monetary Fund might not be perceived as authority figures at all. Specialist knowledge is needed to comprehend any of their work, and without it their contributions to public debate can be literally incomprehensible. Recall that people who score higher on authoritarianism prefer clarity, certainty, and concreteness. They are naturally sceptical towards niche knowledge.

A number of studies have suggested that people who score high on authoritarianism are more likely to believe in conspiracy theories. In other words, they are more likely to be suspicious that powerful actors are trying to deceive them with sinister intent. They are particularly prone to suspecting ill of non-government entities and disliked out-groups (Wood & Gray, 2019).

Telling them that they should distrust technocrats, ivory-tower policy wonks, or people 'from organisations with acronyms' is almost unnecessary. They are doing so already.

Voters who score higher on authoritarianism are not less intelligent, they are just more cautious. They prefer order rather than originality. As we have discussed, lateral thinking is particularly anathema to them. As reassuring messages go, 'Brexit means Brexit' is in exactly the type of format that Leave voters prefer. It is lucid in its reductionism, and straightforward in its logic.

Don't mess with Brexit. End of.

Take Me to Your Leader

Deep in the heart of any authoritarian is a loyalty to the leader, regardless of who that leader happens to be. It is often said that leadership is less a capacity to show the way, and more the ability to make other people do things. In other words, leaders succeed not by showing leadership, but by cultivating followership.

In any event, leadership can mean different things in different situations, and at different times. One of the earliest descriptions of the psychology of leadership was when 19th-century historian Thomas Carlyle argued for his 'Great Man theory' (Carlyle, 1841). This theory sees leadership as involving superior intellect, heroic courage, divine inspiration, and good breeding. That last point reflects the view that leaders are born and not made. Another quite conspicuous element of the theory related to what gender the best leaders should be. The clue is in the title.

Empirical research has confirmed that both intelligence and confidence help people in leadership roles (Judge, Bono, Ilies, & Gerhardt, 2002). There is even some data suggesting that leadership skills are genetically heritable, in that twins who both become leaders often display similar styles (Arvey, Rotundo, Johnson, Zhang, & McGue, 2006). However, there are many explanations for this, and research to date has produced little to suggest that leaders are indeed born as opposed to made.

These days we tend to appreciate that different skills are useful for different leadership positions. Psychology research often distinguishes between having a task focus and having a relationship focus (Tabernero, Chambel, Curral, & Arana, 2009). Leaders who focus on tasks—on 'getting things done'—are usually more suited to situations where everything is under control (which allows them to sit back at let things happen) or where everything is absolutely *out* of control (where they can step in and impose order).

By contrast, leaders who focus on relationships are usually more effective when things are *moderately* under control. The idea is that personal relationships and group cohesion are more relevant where conditions wax and wane.

International research suggests that some leadership skills are universal. An example is communication ability. However, others are culturally bound. People in non-Western countries often value leaders who focus on collaborative approaches, while those in Western countries prefer leaders who are good at uncertainty avoidance (House, Hanges, Javidan, Dorfman, & Gupta, 2004). In other words, Western leaders are expected to be good at keeping their more authoritarian voters happy.

For Brexit it might be said that conditions have been anything but under control. In that regard, while everyone is losing their heads, it is important that the leader remain task-focused. Through most of the Brexit saga this was the job of Prime Minister Theresa May, a leader who struck many observers as taking the notion of task focus to new levels. Relationship-oriented she certainly was not.

It was journalist John Crace who christened her 'Maybot,' a way of conveying her ultra-mechanical approach to whatever task lay before her, and her manner of producing the same reactions to every situation—literally, at times, responding to different question with precisely the same answer (Crace, 2016).

Oxford psychology professor Dorothy Bishop speculated that May's behaviour was similar to that of a person who had been brainwashed. Her unremitting schedule had deprived her of time to think things through, caused her physical exhaustion, and locked her into a mental set as a means of coping, a monomania from which she couldn't escape (Bishop, 2019).

While May was famous for being dutiful, hard-working, and self-contained, she was also known for being introverted, anti-charismatic, and a stilted communicator (Rawnsley, 2019a). Her rivals, on the other hand, were the complete opposite of all these things.

Where May was monochrome, others were colourful. In the broader world of Brexit, virtually every other character with a leadership role or ambition has been conspicuous in being, well, *conspicuous.*

The Leader of the Opposition, Jeremy Corbyn, shot to prominence with a famed rebellious streak, a true Westminster non-conformist, and a frequenter of rock festivals and organic farming allotments (Edwardes, 2017). We have already alluded to UKIP leader, Nigel Farage, widely seen too to be a maverick, albeit in different ways to Corbyn (unlike the vegetarian Labour leader, Farage can be expected to enjoy his steak well done).

Conservative MP Jacob Rees-Mogg, while merely the deputy to a leader (of the European Research Group, a Conservative Party caucus), still projects an eccentricity in mannerism, diction, and wardrobe that has become truly renowned. An acolyte of traditional English history, he is famously referred to by friends and foes alike as 'the Honourable Member for the 18th Century' (Lusher, 2017).

And Conservative leading light, Boris Johnson MP, one-time Foreign Secretary and perennial leadership aspirant, is vividly larger than life. He is frequently heard quoting Latin, telling jokes, and cultivating a carefully constructed roguish media image (Purnell, 2014). When promoting his suitability as Prime Minister, the best that one of his colleagues could come up with was that he had 'oomph', a quality that is, apparently, highly desirable (Owen, 2019).

Self-caricatures can prove to be very useful costumes. Sometimes they provide camouflage, other times they serve as high-vis vests. The occasional administrative faux pas or offensive remark can be written off as a side-effect of individualism, something that goes with the territory when you have your own mind. On the other hand, being a distinctive character guarantees that the public will always remember you, even if they don't quite recall what you stand for.

Difference catches the eye and sticks in the mind. An attractive personality can be particularly good at attracting votes—even from voters who might not agree with, or remember, your views.

These days, it also pays to be emotionally intelligent. In the past, people wished that leaders would be stoical and firm. A stiff upper lip was something to be desired in a politician. However, in the mid-1990s, Western culture came to welcome public displays of emotions and emotional styles of interaction. Political leaders, especially across the English speaking countries (Blair, Clinton, Cameron, Obama, along with Ireland's Bertie Ahern), became regarded as much for their affable empathy as for any economic competence, strategic astuteness, or calmness under pressure.

This freeing of emotions into the political and professional arena was also reflected in the interests of political scientists and philosophers, a shift in cultural studies that has been referred to as the 'affective turn' (Degerman, 2018).

One striking element of all this is that, culturally, emotions are seen as the enemy of reason. Emotions are said to interfere with the soundness of decision-making. They promote a kind of irrationality. As such, when voting for leaders *because we see they are emotional*, it could be said that we are choosing to elect candidates on the basis that we believe them to be irrational.

In the past we sought leaders who could restore the economy or protect us from a foreign adversary. Nowadays we are happy with someone who will cry with us, who is good at playing the role of angry underdog, or who is all about the LOLs.

Except if you are a woman. In political leadership, as everywhere else, women are judged by different standards (Dolan, Deckman, & Swers, 2017). They are frequently criticised for leadership styles that attract praise when adopted by men (Eagly, Makhijani, & Klonsky, 1992). Women politicians who acquire reputations as serial polygamists, or who appear on television with their shirt hanging out and their hair unbrushed, are rarely indulged with the excuse that they are charming and interesting.

But perhaps the greatest sexism faced by Theresa May was the very fact that she became Prime Minister in the first place. After all, the vacancy she filled—leader of a country that had just been plunged into chaos—hardly seemed all that attractive. Such is so often the way of things. Research suggests that women often end up in leadership roles at times of particular hardship. They are put in charge when failure seems a strong possibility. The effect is so common that it has a name: the 'glass cliff' (Ryan & Haslam, 2007).

Perhaps because more of the male in-group are reluctant to put themselves forward for risky duties, women find that a period of chaos usually presents their best chance to assume a leadership role. We can note that when Theresa May became leader, the second candidate being considered in this two-person process was also a woman, pro-Leave MP Andrea Leadsom.

It might all be a coincidence, of course. But it would not be the first time a male hierarchy decided that the very moment the ship begins to sink feels like a good time to let one of the women take over.

II. Groups Matter

Talking about Leavers and Remainers does not advance much past the ecological fallacy. To say that Leavers 'have higher scores for authoritarianism' is to risk the same type of over-generalisation. It is important to remember that the group average for Leavers does not apply to every person in that group. There are many different types of Leaver, as there are many types of Remainer. One size does not fit all.

But sometimes it makes sense to consider the psychology of groups as single entities. For example, it makes sense to ask whether groups develop such levels of cohesion that the people within them begin to lose their sense of individuality. It also makes sense to ask about the dynamics of inter-group conflict: why do groups divide from each other in ways that create tension?

The Hive Mind

There are many situations where a group can solve a problem, make a better decision, or answer a question more effectively than an individual. This is the basis of crowdsourcing. Inputs can be garnered from large selections of the general public in the hope that their combined efforts will produce superlative intellectual firepower.

However, there is not always wisdom in a crowd. One problem is the multiplication of noise. When a group is large, in theory this should widen the range of its suggestions, guesses, estimates, or ideas. The very best outputs should be produced. However, that theory only holds if individual group members work independently.

In real-life group dynamics, people often check in with what others are saying. They are influenced by what they hear, succumbing to a cascade of psychological consequences that defeat the purpose of collaborating (Lorenz, Rauhut, Schweitzer, & Helbing, 2011). Small errors easily become magnified. Consensus drifts far from correctness. Arbitrated conclusions are not necessarily accurate.

When people begin to compare views, the range of their suggestions narrows rather than widens. People feel inclined to work towards a consensus, but not on the basis of reason and evidence. Rather, they are influenced by mutual reinforcement.

As we saw in Chapter 2, pluralistic ignorance takes hold. People reinforce what they think should be reinforced, simply on the basis that they witness other people reinforcing it. A room full of nodding heads might look reassuring, but only if you ignore the fact that nodding is actually contagious.

When groups form naturally, they often do so in ways that make all these problems worse. People tend to seek the company of like-minded soul mates. They spend time with others who they know agree with them about the things they care about most (Hart et al., 2009). They then receive falsely narrow feedback regarding the accuracy or acceptability of their own views. Gradually they cultivate an erroneous sense of the world around them.

Smokers overestimate the number of smokers in the population, while non-smokers overestimate the numbers who do not smoke. People who drink alcohol overestimate how much alcohol other people drink; teetotallers do the opposite (Cunningham, Neighbors, Wild, & Humphreys, 2012). Europhiles spend all their time with other Europhiles, then are shocked upon discovering that a majority of their compatriots think differently to them.

When your primary source of comparison is a community of people just like you, your exposure to social opinion will be highly selective. When groups form, they quickly harden. This is the way of the echo chamber.

Echo, Echo

In one particularly detailed evaluation, researchers in the United States studied the behaviour of over 3.8 million Twitter users, during and after a selection of political and non-political events (Barberá, Jost, Nagler, Tucker, & Bonneau, 2015). The researchers tracked the patterns of retweets that were posted by these users, creating a statistical model showing the way information flowed through what was a vast network of user-to-user connections.

Twitter users often try to emphasise the point that 'a retweet is not an endorsement.' However, the very existence of such a disclaimer is a sign of the fact that more of than not, it is. In all, the researchers tracked 150 million retweets. They did not assess the content of individual posts, which would require a lot of text analysis and subjective judgement. Instead, they wanted to find out how extensively people produced and shared information between selective groups, thereby limiting its visibility. They classified each user by political preference, based on their Twitter profile. For example, they checked to see if a user followed other accounts that promoted political causes or positions.

The researchers found that for non-political events, like the Oscars, users shared tweets in a generally open way. But during political events, such as election campaigns, they clearly prioritised material from politically like-minded sources. The overall effect was to create swarms of mutually-reinforcing tweets that flowed through Twitter within ideologically segregated user communities. As time went on, and as users retweeted tweets that had already been retweeted by others, the increasing intensity of within-group interactions made the sub-groups more and more homogenous.

By and large, during such events, users subdivided into two major clusters. It seems true that social media does indeed operate as an echo chamber.

Importantly, these researchers also found that users classified as conservative (on the basis of being more likely to follow conservative accounts) were more prone to this echo chamber effect. They engaged with like-minded others to a greater extent. This may reflect the idea that people who score high for authoritarianism prefer conformity, and are generally less comfortable with difference. They are more inclined to seek, and to provide, reinforcement for their own views (Stern, West, Jost, & Rule, 2014).

Social media echo chambers are a prominent feature of Brexit. In an analysis of 7.5 million tweets posted during the referendum, it was found that Leave-related tweets outnumbered Remain tweets by a ratio of around two-to-one. In addition, Leave voters were far more likely to interact with other Leavers—by replying, retweeting, or quoting—than to interact with Remainers (Hänska-Ahy & Bauchowitz, 2017).

Brexit-related echo chambers on Twitter exhibit discernible geographic dimensions. Leave supporters are more likely to interact with fellow Leavers who live close to them, whereas Remainers are more likely to interact with users who live further away (Bastos, Mercea, & Baronchelli, 2018).

Leavers conduct more Brexit-related Google searches, and post more intensively to both Facebook and Instagram, compared to Remainers (Herrman, 2016). A study of more than 1 million Facebook accounts showed that users quickly self-segregate into sharply polarised Leave and Remain echo chambers when interacting with syndicated news posts (Del Vicario, Zollo, Caldarelli, Scala, & Quattrociocchi, 2017).

The danger with echo chambers is that they are breeding grounds for 'groupthink'. Groupthink occurs when agreement becomes more valuable than accuracy, and the desire for mutual reinforcement overrides people's ability to realistically appraise the world around them. It can foster irrational and suboptimal decision-making in even the most well intentioned people.

Research suggests that groupthink is most likely to arise where groups are homogenous, cohesive, isolated from outside option, and intuitive. Groupthink discourages people from seeking alternative views, or from assessing risk. It makes crises happen, and then it makes them worse.

The problems associated with groupthink are best tackled head on, by bringing people with diverse positions together so they can experience perspectives different to their own. Deliberate effort is required. As we have seen, human beings are just not inclined to do this type of thing by themselves.

Leaders who want to avoid making bad situations worse would be well advised to do everything they can to break down the walls of the echo chamber. Unify voices. Promote perspective-sharing. And at all costs avoid the risk of group polarisation.

That would be ideal.

Poles Apart

In July 2016, when launching her candidacy for leader of the Conservative Party, aspiring Prime Minister Theresa May delivered the speech in which she asserted that 'Brexit means Brexit' (and she was going to make a success of it). As May had campaigned for Remain, it is tempting to believe she felt a particular need to emphasise her full-blooded commitment to the Brexit cause.

Psychologists refer to 'cognitive dissonance', the discomfort a person feels when they have two conflicting ambitions or values. People respond to dissonance in different ways, but many seek to conquer their stress by maximising their conviction. Hence we see the phenomenon of the zealous convert—the person who becomes a fervent evangelist for their new point of view, if not indeed an extremist.

As discussed in Chapter 2, the Brexit referendum did not seek to specify the dimensions of what 'leaving' the European Union would involve. There was no mention of when exactly the United Kingdom would depart. There was no reference to the single market or the customs union, both of which Britain could continue to avail of after ceasing to be an EU member.

But soon May had determined that Brexit meant everything, lock, stock, and two smoking barrels. In her speech to the Conservative Party conference in October, she emphasised that speed was of the essence: the Article 50 process, the formal procedure for withdrawing the UK from the European Union, would be triggered at the earliest opportunity.

Political rivals who wanted to delay Brexit were 'insulting the intelligence of the British people,' she said, an early example of the ecological fallacy on Brexit manoeuvres (Dominiczak & Wilkinson, 2016). She declared a red line on jurisdiction of the European Court of Justice. In a pivotal January speech in Lancaster House, she stated that Britain would leave both the single market and the customs union. By and large, May is said to have made most of these announcements without alerting her cabinet colleagues in advance (Shipman, 2017). This zealous convert was in a hurry.

May's strategy sought to implement Brexit to maximum effect, apparently making no allowance for the fact that only a slim majority of voters had approved the referendum. But then referendums are, by their nature, binary. They have just one outcome. There is no provision for diluting the verdict of a referendum on the basis of the closeness of its result. Nonetheless, the Prime Minister's approach undoubtedly served to alienate those who had voted, and campaigned, for Remain.

While it was legitimate for the Prime Minister to think only of the side that won, her strategy had the effect of creating an echo chamber of self-reinforcing in-group reasoning. It promoted hasty and uncritical thinking within her tribe. It also raised tension by maligning the legitimacy of her adversaries.

In April 2017, May called a snap general election, despite previously having undertaken not to do so. Opinion polls had proved too tempting. They had suggested that the Conservatives could increase their majority and thereby strengthen their stranglehold on Brexit. That this was the standard media narrative of events served only to deepen the public's sense of polarisation. The Prime Minister of the day was opportunistically seeking to capitalise on popular sentiment in order to obliterate her political rivals.

As things turned out, her electoral strategy backfired. The Conservatives in fact *lost* their parliamentary majority. Now they could only form a government with the cooperation of Northern Ireland's Democratic Unionist Party. The Democratic Unionists had many esoteric policies. Among their number were anti-Darwinists, Young Earth creationists, and Biblical literalists. In Northern Ireland, they had once appointed a climate change sceptic to the post of environment minister.

As well as humiliating the new May government, the election result greatly diluted its mandate. What had been a clear majority—and a constitutional licence to make decisions for the country unassisted—had now become a quagmire. Technically, the government could only take action if the ten Democratic Unionist MPs allowed them to.

While the new parliamentary arithmetic might have encouraged, if not forced, a more collaborative approach, if anything May doubled down on her Brexit-at-all-costs strategy. Leading a minority administration in a hung parliament appeared to make no difference.

This is as much a product of the United Kingdom's political system—the custom and practice encoded by the mother of parliaments—as it is any flaw innate to the character of Prime Minister May. As political journalist Andrew Rawnsley (2019b) has described:

> This is not just because Mrs May is a rigid and unimaginative character. She is the product of a political culture that tends to emphasise the adversarial over the consensual. It is expressed in the architecture of a parliament that sits the two sides confronting each other. European countries with more experience of coalition governments are schooled in the art of the compromise. The idea is foreign to the winner-takes-all tradition of British politics.

Research in psychology has suggested that when groups are polarised they tend to adopt attitudes that are exaggerations of the average opinions of their members. Over time, this process leads to sentiment escalation.

First, people are concerned about the curvature of bananas, then they want to leave the European Union, then they want a 'soft' Brexit, and after that they want a 'hard' one. By the time they are about to elect a new leader for their party, with just months to go before the deadline for departing, the major candidates for leadership openly talk about leaving the EU with no deal at all. This, they believe, is where their group as a whole are now at.

Such escalation results from a combination of psychological effects. One problem is the way individual group members feel the need to convince others that they are suitable to be part of the group. When they hear a particular attitude, they tend to offer it back plus ten per cent. This reaction, a kind of bandwagon effect, has been called 'normative influence' (Von Swol, 2009).

A second aspect is that, when you confine your discussions to like-minded others in an echo chamber, you will likely only ever encounter arguments in favour of your own starting position. Some of these arguments will be ones you hadn't heard before. Therefore, the result of discussion is that you end up with more arguments in favour of your position that you started with. And so you end up more convinced than ever. This leads to an upward spiral of fervour, conviction, and zeal, in a process known as 'informational influence' (Turner, Wetherell, & Hogg, 1989).

A third component is a very human instinct: the wish to avoid standing out from your peers. Only a minority of humans feel comfortable being the odd one out. Most people form a view of what the typical member of a group looks like, and then try to conform to that prototype. As a result of the availability heuristic, the most striking examples of group behaviour will loom larger in the mind. Consequently, the power of social conformity serves to accentuate the group's attitudes over time (McGarty, Turner, Hogg, David, & Wetherell, 1992).

Group polarisation, by its nature, is a problem that only gets worse. When people come to identify strongly with a particular group, they often feel they must go beyond merely advertising their membership of it. Not only must they feel proud of their own group, they must also think ill of other groups. This is exacerbated by the problem of out-group homogeneity that we discussed in Chapter 2. As things spiral further, soon it feels right to start defending your group from rivals.

And of course, often the best form of defence is attack.

When polarisation sets in, you know it is time to get paranoid.

Deal or No Deal: Parliamentarians as Prisoners

In Chapter 2 we saw how Prime Minister Theresa May struggled to get her withdrawal agreement through Parliament. Her exasperation led her to produce 'the single worst speech she has ever given.' May had identified the passing of the Withdrawal Agreement Bill as her career-defining objective. Unfortunately, her efforts to define her career this way proved monumentally unsuccessful.

The first so-called 'meaningful' vote on the bill was originally scheduled for December 2018. However, after it became apparent that a hundred Conservative MPs planned to vote the deal down, the vote was postponed (Sabbagh & Elgot, 2018). When the deal eventually came before Parliament in January, a total of one hundred and eighteen Conservative MPs rejected it (Stewart, 2019). It was the biggest rebellion against a Conservative Prime Minister since John Major was thwarted by 95 of his colleagues when attempting to pass gun-control measures in 1997 (Scott, 2019).

More significantly, the scale of defeat for the government—a losing margin of 230 votes—set a new standard for parliamentary failure. It smashed the previous record, a defeat of 166 votes for Labour Prime Minister Ramsay MacDonald, which had stood for ninety-five years (Edgington, 2019). MacDonald had had the ignominious distinction of not only suffering the worst parliamentary defeat in history, but also the second worst—*and* the third worst. Now Prime Minster May had displaced him at the top of the charts.

A second meaningful vote was held in early March. This time only seventy-five Conservative MPs rebelled, reducing the overall margin of defeat to 149 votes. This was merely the *fourth* worst ever rejection of a government motion. The chart for the top five worst Prime Ministerial defeats now read: May; MacDonald; MacDonald; May; MacDonald. The Prime Minister was certainly making a mark on history.

The third meaningful vote took place on March 29, the day that had originally been set aside for Brexit itself to happen. May promised to resign if the deal was passed (Stewart, Mason, & Walker, 2019), an indication of how perversely contorted the machinations of British politics had become. Despite offering her colleagues the incentive of being able to unilaterally terminate her political career, she was once again unsuccessful. The withdrawal agreement was rejected for a third time, on this occasion by 58 votes. No new records were set.

No negotiation ever fully satisfies any of the negotiators. This is the very nature of negotiating. Compromises are essential. Some desired outcomes must be sacrificed so that others can be achieved. The withdrawal agreement May negotiated with the European Union was certainly a case in point.

Among its most thorny compromises were the proposed arrangements for Northern Ireland, the so-called backstop. This plan would effectively place the United Kingdom in an indefinite customs union with the EU should it prove impossible to formulate a future trade agreement between Britain and the Europeans. Northern Ireland, but not the rest of the UK, would continue to be bound by the European Union's goods regulations. Many Eurosceptic MPs argued that these arrangements would prevent Britain from developing its own independent trade policy, and drive a wedge between Northern Ireland and the rest of the United Kingdom (Blitz, 2019).

But while many MPs, literally hundreds, voted against May's deal, a large number—in fact, hundreds again—vote in its favour. This suggests that, notwithstanding its unpopularity, it was technically possible to support it. It was feasible to defend it with arguments. It was reasonable to conclude that, despite its shortcomings, its advantages outweighed its costs.

The fact that the Withdrawal Agreement Bill was defeated heavily in three meaningful votes reflects the overall *preference* of MPs, a matter of taste and choice. There was no technical stricture that prevented the bill from being passed.

This point here is that MPs could have chosen differently if they were willing to ally themselves to different arguments. This makes their behaviour a psychological consideration. The question is: why did some MPs vote against a bill that others, including many of their closest colleagues, saw as supportable? Its flaws alone were not decisive. In the end, strategy and choice held sway.

One way to explain the impasse is by using what psychologists refer to as 'game theory' (Myerson, 1991). Game theory purports to explain why two rational parties might decline to cooperate even though doing so would be in their best interests. To explain the theory, psychologists typically refer to a rather famous puzzle called the prisoner's dilemma.

In the puzzle, a serious crime has been committed. Two suspects are arrested together but carted off to be interrogated separately. Prosecutors have some evidence to charge both with lesser misdemeanours, but not enough to convict them of the serious crime. Therefore, they decide to offer both the same deal. Each suspect is told:

- If you both stay quiet, you will go to jail for *one* year based on the evidence we have thus far.
- If you confess and snitch on your friend, we will drop all charges against you, and pin it all on your friend. Your friend will go to prison for *ten* years.
- However, if your friend confesses *as well*, then technically we won't need you to snitch on each another—your confessions will be enough for us to send you *both* to prison, for *eight* years.

The prisoner's dilemma requires you to imagine being one of the two suspects. Should you stay silent? Or should you snitch?

If you keep shtum then you will go to prison for one year (if your friend keeps quiet as well) or for ten years (if your friend blows the whistle on you). If you confess, then you could go free (if your friend stays quiet) or to prison for *eight* years (if your friend confesses too). In short, silence means one or ten years in jail, whereas snitching means zero or eight.

The dilemma here stems from the fact that you cannot be sure what your friend will do. They have to face the same dilemma as you. That said, snitching on your friend offers a greater reward than staying silent: after all, *zero or eight* years seems much more preferable than *one or ten* years. Betrayal is more attractive than cooperation.

The prisoner's dilemma can be used to help explain the impasse in Parliament over the Withdrawal Agreement Bill (TLDR News, 2019). Instead of two suspects, we have two blocs of MPs, namely, Remainers and Leavers. Their choices can be summarised as follows:

- If they both go along with what is proposed, then the Withdrawal Agreement Bill will be passed, and the negotiated deal, including all its bad bits, will take effect.
- If one side rejects the Withdrawal Agreement Bill then it might be renegotiated to include concessions that that side wants, in order to secure their support in a future vote.
- However, if the other side rejects the Withdrawal Agreement Bill *as well*, then technically all hell will break loose, and a 'No Deal' Brexit will loom on the horizon.

As with the prisoners, both Remainers and Leavers could cooperate and agree to vote for the deal. Everyone would end up with a mediocre outcome that is not something they really want, but is an outcome nonetheless. However, neither Remainers nor Leavers want to take the risk of cooperating. This is because doing so might provide the other side with the opportunity to secure concessions for themselves by voting the deal down.

Therefore, all-out rejection of the Withdrawal Agreement Bill becomes the most likely outcome. A 'No Deal' Brexit becomes the equivalent of eight years in prison, instead of ten. Betrayal trumps cooperation.

This psychological analysis show that votes on the withdrawal agreement are similar to a nuclear arms race. It is in the interests of everyone for both sides to disarm, which would secure peace and save the considerable financial costs of an arms programme. However, as neither side can trust the other to do the right thing, both will choose to accumulate a nuclear arsenal. The more expensive, and potentially more disastrous, course of action becomes the rational choice.

One of the costs of creating a *them-and-us* dynamic at the heart of Brexit politics has been to ensure that exactly this type of stasis is always more, rather than less, likely.

Identify Yourself

Psychologists often point out that human beings have two types of self-image. First, you have a personal identity, your individual characteristics and attributes, your family status, your job, your temperament, and your tastes.

But importantly, you also have a social identity—in fact several social identities—those aspects of your 'self' which relate to the many groups that you belong to. The most obvious groups include your nationality, your ethnic group, and sometimes your town or region. If you belong to a religion, then for many people that will be another important aspect of your social identity.

Several groups emerge from tastes and leisure, such as whether you are a fan of a particular sports team or musical genre. Many people will also have political affiliations, placing them in yet more groups. These may relate to the parties they support, or to their social attitudes—such as whether they consider themselves to be environmentalists, libertarians, monarchists, or feminists.

We all belong to many groups. Whenever we are asked to describe ourselves, we soon start referring to them. While scientific psychology is the study of the individual, quite often individuals consider their own psychologies to be bound up in the groups they belong to. Human beings have a perennial need to identify themselves in tribal terms.

It is true that many people prefer to live isolated lives. They wish never to have a family, never to join a club, never to socialise. They relish spending time alone with their thoughts. But even those very thoughts that they spend time with—the inner monologues with which they speak to themselves—take the form of human language. And language is an inherently communicative experience. Words only have meanings in the sense that more than one person understands them.

Psychologically, we cannot even *think our own thoughts* without resorting to a behaviour that only ever evolved because of our desire to affiliate.

Even if we go out of our way to avoid social interaction, our group identities still complete the definition of who we are. To that extent, our self-perception is somewhat dependent on external circumstances. It is shaped by events and by the wishes of others. While you get to decide if you are a Leaver or a Remainer, you do not get to decide to totality of what being a Leaver or a Remainer means. In technical terms, we self-categorise only to depersonalise.

Many psychologists argue that human behaviour is critically determined by social identity dynamics. Such approaches, often referred to as 'social identity theory', help explain why people behave in ways that romanticise or aggrandise their preferred group. As people identify themselves with their group, it is in their interests to see their group in purely positive terms. Groups provide us with an opportunity to achieve 'optimal distinctiveness' (Hornsey & Jetten, 2004). The rose-tinted glasses effects that we discussed in Chapter 2 are not just applied to the self, but to the tribe as a whole.

As such, Leavers and Remainers are motivated to see their group in noble terms, as defenders of righteousness and protectors of their country's destiny. The group's prestige and status are a source of our own sense of self-worth. Not only that, they encourage us to show in-group favouritism, which in turn exacerbates polarisation.

Data from the British Election Study show how group identification can impact on an emotional level (Evans & Schaffner, 2019). As time passes, greater numbers of both Leavers and Remainers prefer to use the term 'we' instead of 'they' when talking about their side of the Brexit divide. More than ninety per cent agree that they have 'a lot in common with other supporters' of their views on Brexit. And when people criticise either the Remain or Leave side, voters are increasingly likely to take offense. Numbers saying such criticism 'feels like a personal insult' have doubled since 2016.

The entire Brexit issue is enmeshed in competing identities. At its core is an existential question about groups: should Britain's citizens be part of a superordinate EU group identity? By and large, psychology research suggests that encouraging people to feel part of a higher-level identity is beneficial. Lessening the fragmentation of society helps to reduce the problems of in-group favouritism and bias. Being part of the same overall group makes us like each other more (Kunst, Thomsen, Sam, & Berry, 2015).

Therefore, how citizens categorise themselves will shape their attitudes to Brexit. Those who identify with a European identity should be motivated to preserve it, while those who do not should be more willing to give it up.

To an extent, this type of analysis might seem obvious and possibly circular. After all, it effectively reduces to a claim that people keep what they like and sacrifice what they don't. But where a social identity approach can be particularly useful is when it is tested alongside other proposed explanations for Brexit.

For example, in one study, researchers surveyed voter attitudes before and after the 2016 referendum. As well as questionnaires that assessed suspected predictors of voting, they asked participants various questions about their perceptions of group identity (Van de Vyver, Leite, Abrams, & Palmer, 2018).

As in previous studies, these researchers found that authoritarianism (which they referred to as 'conservatism') made people more likely to support Brexit. But importantly, group identity—specifically European identity—helped tip the balance. The statistical results suggested that a person's authoritarianism helped to determine their European identity—and that identity helped to determine how they voted on Brexit. In short, personal identity drove social identity, and then social identity drove behaviour.

An important social identity in the psychology of Brexit is that of nationality, ethnicity, and race. At a very simple level, the referendum vote differed across the constituent countries of the United Kingdom. England

and Wales voted Leave, while Scotland and Northern Ireland went for Remain. There are many demographic differences across the four countries of United Kingdom, but it seems likely that their Brexit verdicts were at least partly driven by perceptions of national identity.

Several surveys have given credence to that suspicion. Brexit voters who describe themselves either as 'British only' or 'Welsh only' have been found to divide evenly between Leavers and Remainers. Those who identify as 'Irish or Northern Irish only' show a 55:45 preference for Remain (although this categorisation is complicated by the dual nationality provisions that apply to people born in Northern Ireland). However, voters who identify as 'English only' voted for Leave by a two-to-one majority, while those who identify as 'Scottish only' voted by a similar margin in the other direction (Richards & Heath, 2019).

As such, nationalism per se does not predict Brexit attitudes. Nationalism is not a simple measure. What matters more is the broader social identity, the meanings people attach to their Englishness, Scottishness, and so on. These perceptions of national identity can be expected, in turn, to influence attitudes towards immigration and foreignness, a topic we will return to in Chapter 5.

The Point of It All

Social identity research can always be criticized for relying on surveys, self-reports, and arbitrary statistical models derived from relatively selective datasets. People who fill out questionnaires are often guarded about their true feelings, and sometimes suffer from hindsight bias.

In other words, their recollection of past events—such as what caused them to form their current views—can often be imperfect. While social psychology researchers are keen to measure *what people think*, their methods often get no further than recording *what some people say about what they think they think* (Hughes, 2016).

That said, the social identity approach is extremely important because it draws attention to the very psychological fact that people have multiple 'selves'. In some situations we are of a particular nationality, in other situations we are of a particular profession, in other situations we are of a particular social attitude group, and in other situations we support a particular sports team.

Quite how we see ourselves at any moment depends on who we are inter-acting with, on who our audience is. Our identity of relevance changes as the context shifts. If identities are intertwined with social context, and if the group we feel we belong to varies depending on the situation, then this has important implications for understanding political behaviour (Reicher, 2004).

Much of politics, and indeed much of psychology, is dependent on how we define and evaluate people's self-interest. But if people have multiple 'selves', then what exactly we should be evaluating?

What 'self' should we be thinking of when we talk about *self*-interest?

Ultimately what motivates people, and the groups they form, is an overall wish to feel secure, esteemed, calm, and happy. In rupturing the very norms by which they construct their sense of self, and by pressing reset on citizens' national and pan-national group identities, Brexit has created a powerful test of the resolve for which the British people—ecological fallacy notwithstanding—have become so renowned.

Keeping calm and carrying on might have served them well in the past. In our next chapter, we examine whether a stiff upper lip is still sufficient for dealing with stress in today's Brexit Britain.

4

Brexit Anxiety

I. On Brexit as a Cause of Mental Illness

In May 2017, Prime Minister Theresa May promised the British people nothing less than revolution. She would overthrow the status quo. She would accomplish lasting change. She would transform homes, schools, and workplaces in all parts of the country. Her pledge was earnest and firm. Her plans were extensive.

Specifically, she would be the Prime Minister who finally brought about a much hoped-for 'mental health revolution' in the UK (Savage, 2017). Staff levels in the NHS would change dramatically. Children and young adults would be made more aware of the reality of living with mental health challenges. The number of people receiving long-term psychiatric care would be transformed. And people from minority ethnic backgrounds, whose emotional struggles are all too often compounded by xenophobia and discrimination, would be significantly impacted. As revolutions go, this one was to be suitably all-encompassing.

The irony of course is that Brexit contributed to just about all of these outcomes eventuating in some form. Just not quite the form the Prime Minister had in mind.

© The Author(s) 2019
B. M. Hughes, *The Psychology of Brexit*,
https://doi.org/10.1007/978-3-030-29364-2_4

It sometimes seems as though the entire United Kingdom has suffered an emotional breakdown over Brexit. According to a headline in the *Daily Express*, the result has been nothing less than 'BREXHAUSTION' (Read, 2019).

In fact, the media have been brimming with armchair diagnoses. 'Are you suffering from "Strexit"?' asked the *Telegraph* (Lally, 2019), or 'from Branxiety?' the *Evening Standard* wanted to know (Butter, 2018). The *Guardian* declared that the country was going through a 'Brexistential crisis' (Spicer, 2016). News website Slate offered a stages-of-change model, classically framing Brexit-related grief in five phases: *brenial, branger, brargaining, brepression* (or *debression*) and, finally, *bracceptance* (Kelly, 2016).

A *Spectator* writer likened Brexit to a whole-body shock, specifically the obstetric traumas endured when having a baby:

> …there will be blood. Brexit is going to be painful, like childbirth. It just is. The Leave quacks who promised a brisk and blissful delivery don't have enough diamorphine to dull the nerves. We might need epidurals from the Treasury. We will swear a lot, and not care. It might be rather embarrassing but again, we probably won't care, because we'll be concentrating on the pain. Other countries will look at us and think 'I'm never going through that'. (Thomas, 2016)

The agony of the democratic labour ward, this writer argued, would quickly give way to unavoidable post-vote fatigue, complete with plunging mood and bleak self-questioning (*Why did I ever do this?*). But eventually, he predicted, the British people would learn to re-evaluate these experiences. They might even come to look back on Brexit, with parental pride, as their greatest achievement in life…

However, according to psychotherapists, this type of parental satisfaction with Brexit is for now proving elusive. Instead, they say, the Brexit experience has created monumental upset, leading to unprecedented demand for their services. There has been a new national outbreak, a mass mental malaise.

Brexit anxiety is affecting people all over the land.

The effects were apparent immediately after the referendum, when newspapers reported on the 'queue of patients' lining up for Brexit-related counselling at British clinics (Prynn, 2016). Within days, the *Guardian* described, 'therapists everywhere' were experiencing 'shockingly elevated levels of anxiety and despair,' with mental health referrals 'already [beginning] to mushroom' (Watts, 2016). Psychoanalyst Susie Orbach wrote about how suddenly 'in therapy, everyone wants to talk about Brexit' (Orbach, 2016).

Three years later, and pressure on therapists seems to have worsened rather than improved. 'My practice is packed,' one trauma specialist told the *Guardian* in early 2019, 'and everybody I know, their practice is packed. I'm finding it incredibly hard to find people to refer on to because nobody has any space' (Williams, 2019).

Brexit is often described as posing profound threats to commerce.

But for the psychotherapy industry, at least, it could turn out to be very good for business.

Land of No Hope and Glory

The views and experiences of psychotherapists, along with the opinions of journalists and bloggers, paint only part of the picture. And the part painted will almost certainly be the most subjective. Individual therapists might well report bustling waiting rooms, but it could be that other practices are idle rather than overloaded. The problem is that idle therapists write few op-eds in the *Guardian*.

And even if it is true that 'everyone in therapy wants to talk about Brexit,' that is not the same as saying that everyone has sought out a therapist for this reason. Perhaps these clients would have been in therapy anyway. Having arrived for their therapy session, it is only natural that they would want to discuss the major issue of the day.

In short, anecdotal evidence gives us little to go on when trying to establish the extent, nature, and meaning of Brexit anxiety. The views of therapy providers might be skewed. What draws the attention of journalists might not reflect reality.

To get a better grasp, we need to consider some data.

One problem with this is that Brexit is still in its infancy. Although it sometimes seems like we have had Brexit in our lives forever, the period since the 2016 referendum has been relatively brief. The wheels of research do not turn that fast. It takes time to arrange a study, to enrol participants, to gather and analyse data, and to publish meaningful results.

Mental health research, in particular, is especially gradual. Mentally vulnerable people face many challenges and will often consider research participation to be quite low on their list of priorities. Some will be too debilitated to even try to volunteer. Psychologists know that they need to be patient if they want to study these issues. In the science of mental health, fast research will often turn out to be bad research.

Add to this the fact that Brexit is highly fluid. The political context changes by the month, if not the week, and sometimes by the day. This makes *slow* research all the more complicated. Studies can be out-of-date before they are even properly up and running. And some types of data, such as official healthcare statistics, are released sporadically, maybe only once a year, making it especially difficult to compile fine-grained analyses of how anxiety has (if it has) developed over time.

Nonetheless, with every passing month, more and more data become available. Each dataset might have flaws, but the emerging pattern of findings helps to guide us towards an understanding.

On the basis of what has been produced so far, it seems reasonable to acknowledge that, indeed yes, Brexit anxiety is certainly a thing. While some people are unflappable, others are very much weighed down by Brexit-related turmoil. The stress-load caused by Brexit is significant.

Brexit is a true public health concern.

Our Survey Says

A slew of relevant opinion surveys have been conducted. In the main, commercial surveys are rarely as rigorous as clinical studies. A common weakness is their use of simplistic measures: by asking a small number of direct questions, they sometimes offer only a glimpse of people's mental health experiences.

However commercial surveys often have strengths that help to offset their frailties. One common strength is sample size. Such surveys tend to utilise larger samples than those seen when questionnaire studies are published in academic psychology journals.

Virtually every major commercial survey has revealed strikingly high rates of Brexit-related stress in the general population.

A January 2019 YouGov survey of more than 1700 British adults found that two thirds were either 'fairly unhappy' or 'very unhappy' because of Brexit. Four-in-ten reported that 'Brexit and its consequences' were causing a negative impact on their mental health.

And while more than half of Remain-voting respondents reported that their mental health was suffering because of Brexit, so too did one third of Leave voters (YouGov, 2019a). YouGov found the same findings when they repeated the survey in a larger sample later in the year (YouGov, 2019b).

Even though these participants were not diagnosed by a clinical psychologist or psychiatrist, this type of survey result is still important. Several clinical studies have shown that self-reported mental health is a very useful predictor of actual mental health. When people respond to even a single question about their mental health status, their self-ratings reliably predict whether they will receive a mental health diagnosis in the future (Ahmad, Jhajj, Stewart, Burghardt, & Bierman, 2014).

If anything, people are more inclined to *under*-report mental health difficulties in response to survey questions (McAlpine, McCreedy, & Alang, 2018). In other words, opinion surveys are more likely to undercount, rather than overestimate, the true prevalence of mental health problems in their samples.

Therefore, the fact that one third of Leavers are willing to report to pollsters that their mental health is suffering because of Brexit, a political objective that *they* lobbied for and then secured at the ballot box, is particularly notable.

In March 2019, YouGov collected more data in collaboration with the United Kingdom's Mental Health Foundation, an independent national charity. In a sample of 1800 adults, 21% said they had experienced Brexit-related 'anxiety' during the previous twelve months. Seventeen per cent said that Brexit had caused them 'high levels of stress' (Mental Health Foundation, 2019). These subtleties are of clinical interest, because psychologists usually differentiate carefully between anxiety and stress.

'Stress' refers a person's reaction to identifiable external pressures. It relates to the way the body—which includes the brain and all the systems that create emotions—responds to the disruption of its resting state. Stress is often a healthy reaction to a challenging event, although persistent stress can wear a person down eventually.

'Anxiety' refers to an emotional state where a person becomes chronically apprehensive. They worry about the possibility of future stress all the time. Anxiety can be triggered by stress, but often arises independently of it. Anxiety also persists even after a stressful challenge has been dealt with.

The Mental Health Foundation survey is interesting because it suggests that around one-in-five British people recognise Brexit to be a stressful event that creates pressure in their lives, while a similar number have developed lasting negative emotions as a result. (The published information does not allow us to establish the degree of overlap, to check how many respondents reported *both* stress *and* anxiety at the same time.)

People appear to have been affected behaviourally as well as emotionally. One-in-five of the Mental Health Foundation's sample reported arguing with family members over Brexit, while 12% had experienced sleep disruption as a result of their Brexit worries.

In terms of the principles of good research design, a weakness with these surveys is their once-off nature. We can see that many people attribute their anxiety to Brexit, but we do not know whether they would have experienced anxiety anyway, even if Brexit had never occurred. This relates to the cause-and-effect conundrum we discussed in Chapter 1. Just because two events have happened together does not mean that one caused the other. Correlation does not prove causation.

In other words, just because we have *Brexit* and *anxiety* does not mean that we have *Brexit anxiety*.

In a hypothetical world—in other words, a world that *does not exist*— we would compare a group of people living in a country where Brexit happened to an identical group living in a separate but similar country where Brexit did *not* happen. This second group would be our 'control group'. It would show us the baseline level of spontaneous anxiety that arises in ordinary people. We could then compare this baseline to the anxiety seen in our Brexit group, and infer how much *additional* anxiety occurred *as a result* of Brexit.

Back in the real world, once-off opinion surveys will always lack this type of 'control group' scenario. That hinders them from telling us much about true cause-and-effect. In technical language, we would call surveys of this kind 'descriptive' (in that they *describe* how many people are anxious), but not 'inferential' (in that we cannot *infer* what made them anxious).

One way to circumvent these problems is to conduct a survey twice with the same group of people. This would allow you to gauge each person's anxiety level before *and* after a stressful event. If we found that people had stress-free lives *before* Brexit, but were reporting high stress afterwards, we could attempt to make an inference about cause-and-effect. (Even then, we might still be wrong. Brexit might just have coincidentally preceded the onset of stress, having nothing to do with actually causing it. A control group will always be beneficial.)

In practical terms, it is very difficult to conduct the same survey twice with the same people. It is especially difficult to build a double-survey around a major stressful event. For one thing, you would need to know in advance that the stressful event was going to happen.

Therefore, quite often, the best that we can do to unpick cause-and-effect in once-off surveys is to compare and contrast different sub-groups of participants. For example, all the commercial surveys have found that Remainers are far more likely to report adverse mental health than Leavers. This suggests that Brexit circumstances do indeed influence people's mental well-being. The pattern does not *prove* causation, but it implies that there is at least some link between Brexit and outcomes. We are not looking at random or seasonal shifts in the population's anxiety.

In April 2019, YouGov conducted a further survey, this time in collaboration with the British Association for Counselling and Psychotherapy. This survey had a much larger sample than the others, with nearly 6000 British adults completing its questionnaires. In addition, the questions reflected the expert interests of the BACP. Similarly to the other surveys, this one found that a third of its respondents described their mental health as having been 'hurt' by Brexit. However, the main findings of interest related to sub-group analyses.

Age, income, and political affiliation were each found to influence Brexit anxiety. More than a third of pensioners reported that their mental health was damaged by Brexit, compared to just a quarter of under-25s who felt the same. Similarly, 37% of affluent respondents (those in socioeconomic grades ABC1) reported Brexit-related mental health problems, compared to just 27% of respondents who were less well off (those in grades C2DE). And while one-in-five Conservative or UKIP voters had experienced such difficulties, more than 40% of Labour, Liberal Democrat, or SNP voters did so (BACP, 2019).

The period since the 2016 referendum has seen reportable levels of mental health problems arising in many segments of the British population, where people directly attribute their travails to Brexit. The various patterns of subgroup differences highlight the interconnectedness of mental health with political realities.

In short, these commercial surveys have produced consistent circumstantial evidence of Brexit anxiety.

Need More Data

Commercial surveys are conducted to order, on a once-off basis, with bespoke questions rather than clinically informed diagnostic assessments. As outlined above, surveys become more scientifically robust if they are conducted repeatedly on the same people over time. In fact, this would be a minimum requirement if you want to assess change.

A further improvement would be if, instead of asking questions that explicitly mention Brexit—and thereby risk planting ideas in people's minds—researchers could measure participant mental health more discreetly using, say, a standardised diagnostic questionnaire.

A huge sample would also be a bonus. In fact, the huger, the better.

We have already seen that repeat-surveys are logistically difficult to organise. The necessary enhancements take time. Many of the required resources are expensive. This is why good research is rarely fast. But that is not to say that good research is impossible. Or that it never takes place.

This type of research is so comprehensive it can often only be undertaken as a government-supported national project. As it happens, the United Kingdom is one of those countries where precisely such a project has been established.

The UK Household Longitudinal Study has been running since 2009. Longitudinal studies where participants are surveyed repeatedly over many years are called 'panel surveys'. The UKHLS is currently the largest panel survey in the world.

Head-quartered at the Institute for Social and Economic Research at the University of Essex, and funded by the Economic and Social Research Council, the UKHLS reaches out regularly to 100,000 British residents in 40,000 households across Britain. It gathers information on a vast range of topics. It looks at social attitudes, daily life, economic factors, and health. All of its outputs are available to the professional research community to scrutinise in full detail, the only condition being that they must use it for 'public interest' research.

The UKHLS datasets are released in waves. Given the complexity and scale of the endeavour, it can take years for data to become available. As such, statistics relating to the period of the Brexit referendum have just recently emerged, included in the very latest wave of data releases.

As health and well-being are among its target topics, the UKHLS surveys include several detailed questionnaires that are clinically approved for diagnostic use. One of these is called the General Health Questionnaire. The GHQ is one of the most popular tools that mental health researchers use to screen for psychiatric symptoms of distress (Goldberg & Williams, 1988).

The UKHLS surveys also include measures of 'subjective well-being', a concept often referred to as 'life satisfaction'. All told, the surveys provide lots of relevant statistics for testing whether Brexit anxiety is myth or reality.

One group of researchers have crunched the relevant numbers (Powdthavee, Plagnol, Frijters, & Clark, 2019). They combined clinical statistics with detailed economic and demographic information. Armed with multiple waves of data drawn from tens of thousands of people, they evaluated whether Brexit has indeed impacted upon British mental health.

The researchers found no differences in life satisfaction recorded before and after the Brexit referendum. However, for clinical distress, there was indeed a shift. There was a clear and significant increase in GHQ scores, across the sample, after Britain voted to leave the European Union.

Further insights were garnered when sub-groups were analysed. Based on the political questions in the UKHLS survey, the researchers were able to subdivide the dataset into Leavers and Remainers. This revealed that it was Remainers who were particularly affected by post-Brexit distress. In fact, Remainers on their own accounted for the increase seen in the population as a whole. By contrast, Leavers seemed to avoid post-Brexit distress, instead experiencing a post-referendum jump in life satisfaction.

The researchers then dove deeper into the data. They conducted fine-grained analyses to establish how long-lasting these various effects were. They separated out the data into months, and looked right across the six-month period that followed the referendum. They found that Leavers' life satisfaction scores increased slowly throughout this period, becoming most pronounced five months after the Brexit vote.

By contrast, for Remainers, there was an immediate sharp increase in clinical distress, which did not subsequently subside.

In short, based on one of the biggest study datasets in the world, we now know that Brexit was followed by marked increases in clinical distress among large subgroups of the British people—and that these effects deepened, rather than dissipated, over time.

Drug Machine

A second research group have used a very different type of publicly available dataset to assess the impact of Brexit on people's well-being. Rather than draw on survey methods, these researchers pulled information from the NHS's national GP prescription database, to examine if Brexit had had any effect on antidepressant use in the United Kingdom (Vandoros, Avendano, & Kawachi, 2019). Although they used data collected as part of ordinary medical practice, their study had many features that are commonly seen in sound scientific experiments.

Firstly, like the UKHLS researchers, these investigators sought to make like-for-like comparisons across several time-points. They were able to compare antidepressant usage rates before *and* after the Brexit referendum, an important part of any attempt to establish cause-and-effect.

Secondly, the researchers accessed prescription statistics relating to several different types of medication use. This meant that they could use other drugs as benchmarks to help ensure that antidepressant prescription rates did not simply reflect changes in medical treatments in general. In that sense, the data on other drugs served as a 'control' condition, adding important contextual information.

The researchers studied drug prescriptions for every GP practice in England from 2011 to 2016. They were able to use the statistical technique of regression (described in Chapter 2) to study several factors at once. The dataset included detailed figures on all dispensed prescriptions across the six-year period, broken down by month. It took three years for this information to become available, to be analysed, and to be published in a medical journal. Fast research this was not.

Ultimately, the analysis produced a very clear finding.

Based on month-by-month comparisons, average daily doses of antidepressant medications across the United Kingdom increased, in real terms, after the Brexit referendum. Moreover, prescriptions for all other types of medication *decreased* during the same period. People were being prescribed with more antidepressants at the same time as they were getting *fewer* lipid drugs, insulins, antigout preparations, thyroid medications, or iron supplements.

The *relative* increase for antidepressants compared to benchmark medications was 13.4%. By any standard, this must be seen as a very large shift in monthly prescription rates for any kind of medical treatment.

In other words, the immediate aftermath of the Brexit referendum coincided with a dramatic spike in people being given antidepressants by their local doctors. This statistical finding is the digital-database equivalent of those crowded waiting rooms that psychotherapists had been describing to newspapers back in 2016.

Such detailed analyses—based on a complete national database, involving time comparisons and control conditions, and tested using a statistical regression model—provide something far more robust that any media anecdote.

Given the requirement for careful and thorough data collection, together with the time needed to study changes in population health, we are only just beginning to see scientific research that tells us how Brexit is affecting people's well-being. All studies will have their own particular focuses, as well as their own weaknesses, but with more and more research, we can slowly add detail to our picture of the Brexit experience.

In the end, slow research is certainly worth waiting for.

Economic Instability Is Bad for Mental Health

Of course all of these findings could just be coincidental. Maybe people who are stressed feel inclined to blame Brexit after the fact, even though Brexit had nothing to do with creating their mental state. Maybe Remainers are simply more prone to neurosis, as is their wont, being the millennial snowflakes that they are. Perhaps the UKHLS data is just picking up on a ripple of clinical distress that would have occurred with or without Brexit, for reasons we are unaware of.

And, who knows, when people suddenly went looking for antidepressants after the Brexit referendum, perhaps they were reacting to other events that were happening in the world at that time. After all, July 2016 saw wildfires in California, street protests in Brazil, floods in India, and an outbreak of the Zika virus. The military crises in Ukraine, Syria, and Iraq all escalated. The England football team had crashed out of Euro 2016, ignominiously at the hands of lowly Iceland. *Pokémon Go*, the augmented reality mobile phone game, had gone viral, resulting in widespread pangs of #FOMO.

The United Kingdom's Office for National Statistics reports on national happiness in Britain each year. Their surveys are often quoted as suggesting that British people seemed happier, rather than less happy, after the Brexit referendum (Collinson, 2018).

However, population scores for average happiness will combine both positive and negative emotions. Polarised groups will cancel each other out. Marginal increases in the population average for happiness may mask a range of dramatic emotional reactions occurring in large subsets of citizens. In any event, more recent ONS reports have shown that after many years of steady increases, what had been long-term growth in British happiness slowed down markedly after the Brexit referendum (Booth, 2019).

In other words, when the United Kingdom government publishes its own statistics to show that the British people are doing just fine, we need to take such a position with a large grain of salt.

Political instability and economic uncertainty have long been identified as threats to mental health. There is little doubt that Brexit has produced both. Traditional political norms have collapsed. Parliamentary logjam over Brexit is the new standard. Britain's historic two-party system has fragmented, and populist movements are on the rise. It is widely acknowledged that Brexit could even lead to the break-up of the United Kingdom, with the constitutional status of Scotland and Northern Ireland increasingly being put under the political microscope (Foster, 2017).

Economically, Britain's future is very unclear. As Brexit negotiations founder, the British economy has seen citizens hoarding supplies and businesses deferring their investment decisions. These reactions to uncertainty in turn create even *more* uncertainty (Jackson, 2018).

Prior to the originally planned Brexit date of March 2019, stockpiling by British companies anxious at possible disruptions to the UK's ports system contributed to a sharp decline in manufacturing. It was the worst seen in nearly twenty years, and caused the entire British economy to contract by 0.4% (Isaac, 2019). Brexit is not the only factor that hampers economic growth. But for as long as the timeframe and nature of Britain's exit from the European Union remain unclear, Brexit certainly does not *help* the economy to thrive.

Should withdrawal from the European Union lead the United Kingdom into an economic recession, then the impact of Brexit anxiety can be expected to get even worse. International research has demonstrated that recessions are especially damaging to mental health.

The global recession of 2008 saw suicide rates in Europe increase directly in line with the uptick in European unemployment (Stuckler, Basu, Suhrcke, Coutts, & McKee, 2011). To date, over a hundred large-scale studies of recessions have been completed around the world. Their findings show that countries who undergo economic recessions endure substantially increased rates of mental disorders, substance abuse, and suicidal behaviour. Jobless citizens, and those in precarious employment, are always among the worst affected (Frasquilho et al., 2016).

In England, there were more than one thousand extra suicides during the period 2008 to 2010 than would have been projected based on previous trends. English regions worst affected by unemployment witnessed the biggest increases in people taking their own lives. Statistically, the data suggest that in England, each 10% increase in unemployment brings with it a 1.4% increase in the suicide rate. Around forty per cent of all male suicides in the two years after 2008 can be attributed to the unemployment caused by economic recession (Barr, Taylor-Robinson, Scott-Samuel, McKee, & Stuckle, 2012).

Socioeconomic contraction creates a ripple effect on mental health. Cashflow-poverty, indebtedness, unemployment, financial worry, and pension insecurity are all risk factors for mental disorder (Greenglass, Katter, Fiksenbaum, & Hughes, 2015).

Something like fuel poverty can lead to significant distress. People who struggle to pay their fuel bills are four times more likely to suffer depression than people who can pay such bills easily. Living in a house with an average temperature of 15 °C or colder doubles your risk of mental health problems compared living in one that is 21 °C or warmer (Green & Gilbertson, 2008).

Disruption and shortages in health services will only compound the effects of Brexit on mental health. To date, contingency plans for ensuring continuity of care have been condemned for being unclear and insufficient. Much of the planning responsibility has been foisted on already overstretched hospital trusts. Supply chains cannot be secured if, ultimately, no formal withdrawal deal between Britain and the European Union is signed. And for political, cultural, and regulatory reasons, healthcare workers are likely to leave the British system in ever greater numbers (Godlee, Kinnair, & Nagpaul, 2018).

As the UK authorities make plans for life after Brexit, preparedness for the effects of economic shock will be crucial. The available psychological research strongly suggests that mental health services, especially suicide-related supports, will need particularly urgent prioritisation.

II. On Mental Illness as a Cause of Brexit

Alongside the idea that Brexit is a *cause of* mental ill-health is the frequent observation that Brexit itself is *caused by* mental disturbance. Brexit is said to be a symptom of mental disease, a sign that the British people have gone mad. On occasion it is argued that Brexit is basically a full-blown form of insanity, an illness in its own right.

The metaphor of Brexit as madness has become a standard journalistic trope. Before the referendum, the *Washington Post* branded Brexit an act of looming 'economic insanity' (Samuelson, 2016). More recently, the same newspaper declared the United Kingdom's Brexit strategy to be 'an act of collective madness' and 'an insane way to behave' (Dunt, 2019). In the *Irish Times*, a Cambridge University professor decried Brexit as 'a collective English mental breakdown' (Boyle, 2018). 'After soft Brexit and hard Brexit, we now have mad Brexit,' said a *Guardian* columnist, 'barking mad' (Jenkins, 2018).

The *New York Times* summarised this view very succinctly. 'The United Kingdom has gone mad,' it said. The problem with Brexit, it explained, 'is that you can't fix stupid' (Friedman, 2019).

The Insanity Offence

In law, an insanity defence is used to argue that an accused person is not responsible for their actions because of a relevant psychiatric disease. In politics, the opposite strategy is frequently employed. Adversaries are castigated for being 'insane' in order to convince an audience that they should be blamed, and harshly, for their reckless actions. We might call this latter strategy the 'insanity *offence*.'

The insanity offence is frequently deployed in relation to Brexit. It serves to hobble meaningful debate because it dismisses opposing arguments as intrinsically deranged *ab initio*.

In one BBC television panel discussion, journalist Polly Toynbee was severely criticised by economist Liam Halligan after she repeatedly accused him of being 'insane'. 'You can't keep calling people like me insane, questioning my sanity,' he said. 'I have serious qualifications to talk about this stuff.' In response, Toynbee said that She would call him insane again if he was 'not careful,' before claiming that he was one of a number of 'eccentric economists' who favour a 'no deal' Brexit (Davis, 2018). For many people, of course, 'eccentric' is merely a euphemism for 'insane.'

The use of psychiatric metaphors to demean political opponents has a long history in rhetoric. In the most extreme cases, it has led to systematic abuse by totalitarian states, as a way of suppressing dissent. Even today, political prisoners around the world are frequently detained in psychiatric hospitals, widely believed to be little more than a regime's way to denigrate the credibility of its adversaries (Bonnie, 2002). In democratic countries, the use of psychiatric insults not only reflects the wider social stigmatising of mental illness, it also serves to reinforce it (Beveridge, 2003).

The term 'insane' is no longer used in mainstream psychology. It is considered so laden with stigma as to be truly damaging. Professional associations that represent psychologists discourage its use, and lobby for it to be removed from the legal system (LaFortune, 2018).

However, the insanity offence does not always require direct use of the term 'insane'. Often the implication is made in other ways, such as when political opponents are dismissed for being 'emotional.'

Emotionality is in many senses the new insanity. It enables a politer, more woke form of the insanity offence. It allows people to dismiss unwanted views as emotionally infused whinings driven by 'anger' or 'rage' or 'panic.'

Brexit supporters are jeered at for being irrationally angry, having had their baser instincts riled by demagogues. Those who object to Brexit are depicted as emotionally immature, the 'Remoaners' who are unable to process their disappointment and move on.

Emotionality is seen as a point of permanent divide: *There is no point talking to you when you are like this. And you are always like this.*

Such dichotomies are fuelled by the reasoning problems outlined in Chapter 2. The availability heuristic ensures that the most egregious examples of our opponents' irrationality stick firmly in our minds. Out-group homogeneity bias makes us tar the other side with one brush. And the third-person effect primes us to assume that while we ourselves are balanced and calm, the others are just incapable of thinking straight. They need to calm down.

As we noted in Chapter 3, emotions are classically seen as the enemy of reason. However, in reality, while emotions place pressure on rationality, they do not entirely suppress it. In fact, most psychological perspectives see emotions as central to effective decision-making, at least in some situations. Where decisions relate to social topics, emotions can be especially important (Verweij, Senior, Domínguez, & Turner, 2015).

Clinical studies show that brain-damaged patients who suffer from alexithymia—the inability to express or detect emotions—often do very poorly in standardised tests of decision-making (Damasio, 2005). Emotionality can be so useful for decision-making that many researchers believe Artificial Intelligence can only succeed if it learns to think more emotionally (Martínez-Miranda & Aldea, 2005).

Emotions help us to form views about the relative importance of issues (LeDoux, 2002). Emotions also provide us with the equipment to learn from experience. If we were incapable of positive and negative emotions, then we would never feel good about getting things right, or regretful when things go wrong. In this way, emotions are pivotal to our developing intellect.

The Pathologising of Politics, and the Politicising of Pathology

Concepts of mental disorder abound in the Brexit landscape. They take many forms. Claims of national masochism and self-harm. Allusions to overwhelmed psychotherapy waiting rooms. Repeated use of the insanity offence. Simplistic tribal name-calling. Accusations of emotionality.

Dismissing others as being addled by mental disorder is a highly effective way of undermining their political dignity. It also means that you need not listen to, or engage with, their arguments. Classifying their opinions as psychiatric symptoms has a profoundly delegitimising effect.

A flavour of this can be gleaned from the way Leavers and Remainers interact in the comments sections of British newspaper websites. The following examples of the insanity offence were identified by researchers who studied over 2500 such discussion threads relating to Brexit (Meredith & Richardson, 2019):

- *You have to remember that when you deal with Brexiters you are dealing with fanatics who cannot accept reason and with feeble minded elderly people....*
- *Remainers have shown themselves to be fantasists, delusional idiots...*
- *The remainers should really now get back in touch with reality.*
- *I prefer 'remainiac' to 'remoaner' to be honest, but both fit the bill.*

Unsurprisingly, the researchers found that while both Remainers and Leavers dismissed their rivals' views as disordered, they consistently considered their *own* views to be reasoned and reality-based.

This perspective assumes that mentally healthy people do *not* get emotionally wound up over things like Brexit. Regular 'sane' people stay rational—emotionless—at all times. The implication is that when people *do* become impassioned over Brexit, their response is more *political* than it is psychological. Their anxiety is seen as a political statement.

When Oxleas NHS Foundation Trust arranged counselling sessions for district nurses in South East London and Kent to help them cope with the stress of Brexit, local UKIP MEP Jane Collins was far from impressed (Degerman, 2018). 'People upset by a referendum result should not be offered a free counselling service,' she complained. In fact, in her view, the decision to offer counselling was nothing less than 'an insult to democracy.'

Her argument was that people who suffer depression as a result of Brexit do not deserve to be treated for it. In other words, mental pathologies should be triaged on political grounds in order to determine who should, and who should not, be helped.

After the story was reported on the *Daily Mail*'s website (Stevens, 2016), it is fair to say that contributors to the online comments section were largely supportive of the MEP's assessment:

- *Oh dear, the poor dears are devastated over our country being a democracy.*
- *What's wrong with 'getting on with it' just like we always used to?*
- *What an absolute load of rubbish...poor little didums, come on guys man up, if you cannot face this how do you cope in your jobs?????????*
- *Counselling? Do the country a favour and buy a rickety old stool and a length of rope.*

And so as politics are pathologised, so too is pathology politicised.

One feature of group polarisation is that both sides often hold mirror-image perceptions of the other. With Brexit, the divide between Leavers and Remainers is a case in point. Both groups believe the other to be addled by a kind of madness. They hold no sympathy for one another's emotional upsets. Anxiety, depression, anger, and trauma do not reflect damaging feelings that warrant the attentions of a psychotherapist. Instead mental anguish is a sign of a person's flawed character and bad politics.

The other side are insane.

Do not listen to them.

The New Normal

The pathologising of political upset has the effect of normalising political calm. Claiming that only the mentally troubled become distressed about issues like Brexit implies that the *healthy* reaction would be to stay quiet and accept whatever is happening. Normal citizens do not cause a stir, they 'leave politics to the politicians' (Degerman, 2018). Don't let things get to you. Keep calm. Carry on.

Lie back and think, literally, of England.

Many of the aphorisms in popular psychological advice project a similar tone: *Laughter is the best medicine! Don't worry, be happy! Look on the bright side! Whatever is getting you down, take a deep breath and forget about it! Stay positive!*

A key element of all this advice is: *Focus on the things you can influence!* And, by implication: Leave everything else alone.

This genre of self-help psychology is older than many people realise. Indeed, the term 'self-help' was coined in the title of a bestselling book published in 1859. *Self-Help* by Scottish Calvinist Samuel Smiles sold more copies than that year's two other notable releases—Darwin's *On the Origin of Species* and Mill's *On Liberty*—combined. Darwin himself was one of the quarter of a million Britons who bought a copy (Hughes, 2004).

Smiles's advice to readers was that hard work, moral fortitude, and self-sacrifice would lead to happiness and success. Linking hard work and morality to success was music to the ears of the privileged Victorian middle-classes. It allowed them to conclude that their comfortable status must be the result of their own hard work and morality.

The modern form of Smiles's self-help approach is represented by what has become known as the 'positive psychology' movement. Today's version is a lot less harsh than what was on offer in the nineteenth century. Instead of thrift and effort, positive psychology is more likely to prescribe self-pampering, duvet days, and mindfulness.

Nonetheless, its effect of promoting compliance to the social order remains unchanged. The key to living a stress-free life is to recognise—and accept—your powerlessness in the face of events.

When BBC Radio 4's *PM* show offered listeners advice on how to deal with Brexit anxiety, one of their experts suggested that people 'take control of the things they can control, such as sleeping, eating, exercising, and limiting their exposure to social media' (Degerman, 2019). Through such personal action, it was implied, could people best survive the turmoil of political upheaval. No need to stress yourself out trying to correct social inequalities or undo democratic injustices, then. Leave politics to the politicians.

The politicians themselves regularly avail of the language of positive psychology. All the better with which to discourage dissent. Critics who express scepticism about Brexit frequently find themselves chastised for their 'negativity' (Shrimsley, 2018). They are accused of projecting 'misguided pessimism' about Britain's post-Brexit future (Tombs, 2019).

After then Foreign Secretary Boris Johnson saw his opportunity to quit the cabinet in the summer of 2018, his parting shot was to complain that the Brexit 'dream' was being 'suffocated by needless self-doubt' (Johnson, 2018). When setting out his case to be Prime Minister, he declared: 'Let's be more positive about this. It's time this country stopped being so down about its ability to get things done' (Walker, 2019).

The language of positive psychology has become something of a mainstream dialect. But among psychologists themselves, the approach is increasingly controversial. It is often seen as a form of surreptitious victim-blaming. Promoting the doctrine that positivity leads to happiness is akin to telling *sad* people that they should feel responsible for their own sadness. They are sad because they are bad at being positive.

When positive thinking and forgiveness have actually been studied, they have been shown to frequently backfire. Among other problems, these tactics end up exposing people to the risk of being taken advantage of by others (McNulty & Fincham, 2012). In an excoriating dissection of the field, American journalist Barbara Ehrenreich famously lambasted positive psychology for encouraging people to seek happiness in the status quo, thereby promoting conformity and quashing dissent (Ehrenreich, 2009).

At first glance it might seem useful to teach people how to cope with life. However, training them to ignore the broader social, economic, and political forces that shape their personal predicaments seems a little misplaced.

Using positive self-talk to transcend your daily hassles might be all very well if you have a good salary, but it will be of very little use to someone on the breadline. Getting more sleep at night might help restore your energy levels, but it will do little to pressurise the political classes into resolving the Brexit crisis.

Recall that human emotions are useful for effective and productive decision-making. Being able to be happy and sad is a prerequisite to being able to tell the difference between good and evil. There is nothing essentially abnormal about getting upset over politics.

And so there is nothing abnormal, unhealthy, or, for that matter, undemocratic about getting upset over Brexit.

A Case Study in How to Cause Stress

Psychologists who study stress classically distinguish between *person factors* and *situation factors*. Person factors include a person's natural coping style and their overall level of resilience. Situation factors, on the other hand, are the various features of the stressful event that is happening. Situation factors are just the worst.

Loosely speaking, the factors that make situations stressful are ambiguity, role vagueness, low control, poor quality feedback, inconsistency of reward, interpersonal conflict, low social support, and unpredictability.

For example, a job, life circumstance, or political event will be all the more stressful if it is ambiguous. The uncertainty associated with an event that *might* be good, but which *also might be bad*, is very distressing. Brexit, as it is presented to the populace by the powers that be, is certainly unclear. And so, Brexit is certainly stressful.

Likewise, Brexit involves a high degree of role vagueness. In other words, citizens are generally uncertain about what their personal responsibilities are. Should they take to the streets to express their support for, or displeasure with, Brexit? Or should they leave politics to the politicians? Should they channel their views on Brexit when voting in general, local, or European elections? Or should they focus on other issues?

How should they react if their local MP holds a different view to them on Brexit, or votes on Brexit in Parliament in a way that they don't like? Should they seek to have them deselected, or should they leave well enough alone? The political system produces role vagueness by sending mixed messages to citizens, as well as by denigrating their sense of control over events. All this makes Brexit more stressful than it needs to be.

Brexit has been administered largely within the bubble of arcane parliamentary procedures. These tend to deliver poor quality feedback to the voting citizen. Politicians channel their work through a mire of meaningful votes, eponymous amendments, early day motions, procedural rulings, and party political chicanery. Meanwhile the executive negotiates with their EU counterparts, producing agreements and declarations with backstops, deals, transitions periods, divorce bills, regulatory alignments, and technological solutions.

Members of the cabinet itself are often left waiting for the Prime Minister to tell them exactly what is going on. Journalists, and certainly voters, are among the last to know anything. The absence of smooth feedback channels adds significantly to the stressfulness of Brexit.

In the Brexit saga, the citizens have cast their votes in a referendum, a general election, and in local elections. They have also had their say in the European elections and in a smattering of by-elections. Quite whether all these visits to the polling station have exerted consistent effects on political developments is unclear.

The major political parties are largely split on Brexit. If you vote for either government or opposition, you cannot be sure whether policy will shift in the direction you want it to, or if it will go in an entirely different direction. From the electorate's point of view, the rewards for voting are utterly unreliable. This inconsistency of reward compounds the stressfulness of Brexit.

Brexit has resulted in a great deal of interpersonal conflict, for several reasons already described in this book. Normal social support networks are contaminated by the Brexit toxin. Large numbers of citizens report arguing with friends and family. Even the peaceable ones are bombarded by angry voices whenever they switch on their televisions in search of the latest update on Brexit hostilities.

It is no coincidence that both Leave and Remain campaigners invoke the rhetoric of war to advance their arguments (Walker, 2019). Brexit is propelled by interpersonal conflict. People cannot help but find it all stressful.

And just about the only predictable thing about Brexit is its sheer unpredictability. People are poor at looking into the future at the best of times. But Brexit has taught them to be especially sceptical when peering at their crystal balls.

The nightmare scenarios promised by Project Fear have largely failed to materialise. The outcome of the 2017 general election was essentially the opposite of what was expected. 'Independence Day' has come and gone with no consequence; the specially commissioned 50p coins resplendently displaying its date have had to be mothballed (Hope, 2019). Political leaders who promised to never support the negotiated withdrawal agreement have gone on to vote for it just days after swearing they wouldn't (Bartlett, 2019). Many red lines turn out to have been drawn in erasable ink.

Some of these surprises were fiascos that we can be glad did not happen. But rather than provide comfort, the unpredictability of events has simply drawn attention to the fact that even experts are not exactly sure what will happen next. Danny Dyer was right: 'no-one's got a f***ing clue.'

Inconsistency of realities breeds helplessness, hopelessness, and a sense of being tortured by events. It makes Brexit just about as stressful as things can get.

Withdrawing from the European Union is not inherently traumatic. Yes, it involves change, which as a prospect on its own is often disliked. However, countries frequently undertake major national projects that involved large-scale changes to the lives of citizens.

Exiting the European Union will be disappointing to those who don't want it. But what makes Brexit stressful is not so much the central prospect of leaving a large-scale pan-national consortium, regardless of how its benefits are portrayed. What makes Brexit stressful is the chaotic, shambolic, and often reckless way in which the entire project has been advanced.

Citizens have no reason to feel relaxed about developments. Brexit has all the hallmarks of an extremely stressful life event. It has all those situation factors that psychologists recommend should be minimised or avoided at all costs.

At various stages, the political classes have had the power to do things differently. For that reason you could say that Brexit offers an important teachable moment for psychologists, citizens, and governments around the world. Brexit stands as a case study in *how to steer a major national project in the most stressful way possible*.

A model for others to *not* follow.

5

Learning from Brexit

I. Brexit Perspectives

The fact that critics condemn the catchphrase 'Brexit means Brexit' tells us something about the power of perspective. Usually, it is difficult to disagree with a truism. Truisms are, after all, true.

The standard criticism of a truism is that it is true by definition. It hardly needs to be said. The very fact that it is true is priced into any condemnation. Disagreeing with 'Brexit means Brexit' is the equivalent to claiming that 'Brexit is not Brexit', which in turn can be reduced to: 'is' equals 'is not'. In other words, 'not' is, well, *not* not.

Some people really hate 'Brexit means Brexit.' The expression has been dismissed as a 'meaningless mantra' (Brooks, 2016), 'homespun superannuated guff' (Smith, 2019), a 'slide into mental incompetence' (Fox, 2016), and an aphorism that takes 'empty rhetoric to a new level' (Coward, 2017). At least one academic has indeed attempted to mount the counterargument that, in fact, 'Brexit does not mean Brexit' (Oikonomou, 2017).

Despite this, in March 2019, when one hundred thousand pro-Brexit supporters marched on the Houses of Parliament to protest at the UK's delayed withdrawal from the European Union, thousands of them proudly

© The Author(s) 2019
B. M. Hughes, *The Psychology of Brexit*,
https://doi.org/10.1007/978-3-030-29364-2_5

held aloft 'Brexit means Brexit' placards. Thousands more held similar signs declaring that 'Leave means Leave' (Clark, 2019).

To these citizens, such slogans are by no means gobbledegook. Their format does not create a logical short-circuit. These protesters certainly do not consider themselves stupid, vacuous, or mentally incompetent.

As we discussed in Chapter 3, asserting that 'Brexit means Brexit' reaches beyond the simple definitional point. This punchy three-word phrase is a nuanced expression of distaste for, well, *nuance*. It is a pre-emptive rejection of the pedantic, definitions-oriented, angels-dancing-on-the-head-of-a-pin evasions that feed into the popular stereotype of academic obfuscation. It is a poke in the eye of the over-complicaters.

Support for Brexit is frequently portrayed as a backlash against the establishment. As one Leave-supporting journalist polemically intoned:

> For decades, Britons have been bossed about by a clerisy of administrators and managers and pose-striking know-alls…They crouched behind 'enlightened' attitudes while imposing their views on a populace they claimed to esteem but more truthfully disdained…Even the most docile beach donkey, if repeatedly kicked, will eventually refuse to cooperate. It will bare its long, yellow teeth and walk in the other direction, pulling its tethers out of the sand. So it has proved with the British voters. Get off our backs, they said. Stop goading us. (Letts, 2017)

In many ways, the Brexit vote is some people's assertion of independence not from the European Union, but from what they see as society's self-styled (and self-appointed) influencers. It is a rebellion against the people who are normally automatically deferred to, the ones whose perspectives usually hold sway.

When academics attempt to grapple with the ins and outs of Brexit, they would do well to remember that this group—the privileged elite—actually includes *them*.

Part of living through a polarising crisis is that, more likely than not, you will end up at one pole or the other. For psychologists, whose field attempts to encapsulate the experiences of humanity as a whole, academic polarisation creates real difficulty. When attempting to draw psychological lessons from political events, we need to keep in mind that psychologists themselves are politically minded.

Psychology, itself, is political.

Respect for Authority

Psychology is a science but that doesn't make it objective. Psychologists are as disposed toward bias as anyone else. As the possessors of human brains—those pattern-detecting engines we discussed in previous chapters—psychologists are humanly susceptible to mental shortcuts, peer influences, and the temptation to view the world through rose-tinted glasses.

Psychologists exhibit the same range of personality attributes as other individuals. They are just as prone to polarisation and in-group favouritism as members of other groups. And given that psychologists exhibit the same type of emotional reactions as everyone else—why wouldn't they?—they are as likely as anyone to find Brexit stressful.

Psychologists are people too, just like you and me.

So does this mean that psychologists are intuitively insightful about the thoughts, feelings, and attitudes of ordinary folk, being, as they are, such ordinary folk themselves? Well not necessarily.

In fact, from what we know about the political attitudes of behavioural scientists, it is most unlikely that they possess such automatic empathy. Their ordinariness tends to be relative. It is framed by the norms of their academic echo chamber. And, in the main, those norms lean anti-Brexit.

Take for example the personality trait said to be common among Leavers, the one for which the technical term is 'authoritarianism'. As pointed out in Chapter 3, studies measuring this factor have found Leavers to score about the mid-range. In other words, their authoritarianism scores are not particularly low and not particularly high. By contrast, the scores of Remain voters are low-to-moderate.

So while it is technically correct to say that Leavers 'have higher authoritarianism scores' than Remainers, it is misleading to suggest that Leavers are especially authoritarian.

Secondly, the word *authoritarianism* is negatively loaded. It has connotations of fascism, despotism, and tyranny. To be labelled an 'authoritarian' is to be criticised and insulted. Any normal usage of the term will be condemnatory.

We should recall that personality traits are usually defined in more even-handed language. Extraversion, for example, is neither good nor bad. If you are an introvert, you might wish you were more extraverted; but then if you are an extravert, you might prefer to be a little bit more introverted. Such inklings would simply reflect personal preferences.

Describing people in such terms is not the same as saying they are objectively good or bad. Neither 'extravert' nor 'introvert' is an insult. Such terms do not imply that people so described should be ashamed of themselves.

Moreover, as human beings are evolved organisms, in reality most people will be close to the mid-range on *all* traits. For example, most people are of average height; relatively few are especially short or tall. The fact that the word *authoritarianism* has negative connotations is therefore unfair. Even people who are middling on this trait will end up being described in terms that sound a lot like criticism.

People who actually score high on authoritarianism tend to hold a strong sense of deference toward traditional forms of authority and to be sceptical toward the unconventional. People who score on the mid-range, obviously, are moderately deferential and sceptical. This is where Leave voters tend to be. It should be possible to describe this reality without stigmatising Leavers. Unfortunately, the very name given to this trait— the word *authoritarianism* itself—is linguistically stigmatising. It makes stigma impossible to avoid.

One way to conclude this point is to consider alternative terminology. If authoritarianism reflects a preference for traditional authority and a reticence about anything that threatens the established order, then perhaps we could call it 'conventionalism'. The flipside of this trait, the other end of its spectrum, we could call 'anti-conventionalism'. Then we could point to the research on the personality of Brexit voters and say:

Remainers 'score higher on anti-conventionalism' than Leavers.

The information being conveyed is the same. Only the terminology has been reworked.

None but the Righteous

A similar issue arises with the details of such research. As pointed out in Chapter 3, people with 'high' authoritarianism scores usually prefer straightforward thinking and concrete solutions. But that is a tame way of putting things. The technical jargon used in academic journals is more cutting.

In the native language of academia, it is said that these people exhibit 'cognitive inflexibility' and engage in 'rigid thinking.' Once again, the labels chosen to describe this group seem more than a little insulting.

It is not rare to want things to be clear-cut and comprehensible. Many people prefer concreteness over abstraction. A person who is especially proficient at clearly structured tasks, but who flounders on more esoteric ones, can hardly be said to have a flawed character.

You don't need *that* much cognitive flexibility to come up with some better terminology to discuss all this.

The irony is that when it comes to research and practice, psychologists are frequently praised for the care and attention they give to language. They are renowned for making efforts to ensure their words are inclusive.

As noted in Chapter 4, the term 'insane' is nowadays proscribed. Psychologists have long been discouraged from referring to people as 'committing' suicide, 'suffering from' depression, or being a stroke 'victim' (APA, 1992). Terms such as 'sexual orientation' are preferred to 'sexual preference,' because the latter implies a degree of voluntary choice that says more about the speaker's political views than it does about the relevant scientific understanding or evidence (APA, 2010).

So, in an era of political correctness, why is it that stigmatising language still persists in some areas? Why is it okay to employ harsh-sounding jargon—words such as 'authoritarian', 'inflexible,' or 'rigid'—to describe some people, when neutrally phrased alternative terms are available?

The problem here likely relates to what critics have bemoaned as a 'liberal bias' in academia, especially in academic psychology (Duarte et al.,

2015). In the Western world, very few psychologists are socially conservative.

More than 90% of psychologists identify as 'liberal.' Fewer than one-in-ten call themselves 'conservative.' When asked if they are willing to discriminate against conservative peers—by, for example, turning down their job applications regardless of their qualifications—more than a third of psychologists agree that it is acceptable to do so (Inbar & Lammers, 2015).

It has been argued that psychology's liberal bias affects more than just the hiring practices of universities. For example, psychologists' view of many social issues is said to be refracted through a political lens. Research on topics such as parenting, racism, religion, and public attitudes to criminality can all be hampered by double standards that result from the political assumptions of researchers (Redding, 2001).

Studies of authoritarianism are often criticised on such grounds. Research that links authoritarianism to various kinds of unethical behaviour often employs politically arbitrary definitions of 'unethical' (such as declaring it 'unethical' to prioritise employment over the environment; Son Hing, Bobocel, Zanna, & McBride, 2007). When alternative definitions are used, differences between authoritarian and liberal people disappear. Both are equally willing to misbehave—for example, by dishing out unfair punishment to members of an out-group—when presented with the opportunity (Crawford, 2012).

Of course, social conservative psychologists would say all that, wouldn't they? We should not forget that the history of psychology reveals an overwhelmingly hegemonic white, middle class, middle-aged, male academic field shaped by a century of Euro-American dominance (Hughes, 2016). And psychology's lean to the 'left' is usually described from a US perspective: what Americans refer to as 'liberal' can often appear quite conservative in global terms (Hilbig & Moshagen, 2015).

Nonetheless, the claim that most academics are socially liberal certainly rings true. And the fact that liberals are less likely than conservatives to support Brexit is also apparent. The idea, therefore, that some psychology research might end up maligning Leave voters in a one-sided way does not seem all that far-fetched.

If some psychology research is skewed in a way that makes Brexiteers look bad, then this is not just a political problem for the behavioural sciences. It also presents a problem of accuracy.

The extent to which Leavers are habitually mischaracterised is the extent to which they are misunderstood. Describing them as 'authoritarian', or dismissing them as too addled to think straight about politics, might simply be an unfair, inaccurate, and misleading way to discuss the psychology of Brexit.

For Brexit, as with any other topic, biased science will be bad science.

Beware the Illusion of Perspective

Recall the Dunning-Kruger problem: as ordinary fallible humans, we are liable to overestimate our own capabilities, even when there is clear-cut evidence that we just don't know what we're doing. And recall also the third-person effect: we imagine ourselves to be immune to those biases we believe so afflict other people.

Therefore, if most psychologists are Remainers, we know from psychology itself what their views about the Brexit tribes will be. They will presume Remainers to be reasonable, and believe Leavers to be lacking.

It is one of the greatest challenges in life to imagine yourself to be wrong. Most people are very shy when it comes to genuine self-criticism. In fact, as we saw in Chapter 2, having a sober, uninflated, grounded-in-reality view of yourself could be a sign that you are actually depressed.

Good science is all about meeting challenges. Science itself was invented as a process of finding ways to circumvent the inherent biases in human logic. Before science went mainstream, people's knowledge was shaped by superstition, mysticism, instinct, prejudice, tradition, social stereotyping, kin loyalty, hearsay, and bias. The insight of science was to recognise that gut reactions do not produce good reasoning.

Science proved to be a civilising process because it provided objective evidence that social injustices were simply arbitrary. Claims that men were superior to women, or that Europeans were some kind of master race, were among several found to be baseless. Science can improve the world, but only if scientists leave their assumptions at the door.

One of the key insights from the psychology of Brexit is surely this: the problem of Brexit is one of extreme psychological polarisation. The Brexit tribes are utterly unable to adopt one another's perspectives. That they hold false views about each other is a systematic side effect of human psychology. Permanent impasse is virtually guaranteed because tunnel vision has become the norm.

What seems entirely reasonable to one group drives the other to complete distraction; and yet neither group seems inclined to wonder why. Instead they presume themselves to be unassailably correct, and conclude that their adversaries must be unhinged. Remainers generally hold this view about Leavers. And Leavers generally hold it about Remainers.

For example, Remainers consider it quite fair to propose that Brexit be abandoned midstream. According to them, the referendum result can be ignored without controversy for a number of reasons.

Firstly, they say, hindsight offers new wisdoms about the reality of a post-Brexit Britain. When the facts change, the electorate should be presumed to have changed their minds. Secondly, quite a lot of the people who voted Leave in 2016 have since died. Were the referendum to take place today, the statistical result, and maybe the decision, would be different (Kentish, 2018). And thirdly, that original referendum result—52% Leave, 48% Remain—was, as these things go, quite close. Such a close-run thing cannot be seen as conclusive. Therefore, say Remainers, the Brexit saga can hardly be said to have a rigidly pre-ordained conclusion.

But such an analysis depends entirely on perspective. Consider the issue of the closeness of the referendum. Prior to the result being known, many Remain campaigners had a different view. Speaking to ITV News on the evening of the referendum, Remain advocate and former leader of the Liberal Democrats Paddy Ashdown was adamant that, regardless of its closeness, the impending result must be seen as the final word:

> I will forgive no one who does not respect the sovereign voice of the British people once it has spoken, whether it is a majority of one per cent or twenty per cent. When the British people have spoken, you do what they command. Either you believe in democracy or you don't.

However, that was when Ashdown believed the Remain side was going to win (Lawson, 2018). After the referendum, he eventually supported calls for a re-run, recommending that the government 'return to the people and beg for a solution' given the 'stalemate' produced by the original outcome (Ashdown, 2018).

Perspective can be a powerful bias. Often the best way to consider its power is to imagine a counterfactual—a scenario that is the opposite of the present state of affairs. This is akin to the approach of falsification, discussed in Chapter 1, which gives the scientific method much of its strength.

The appropriate counterfactual here would involve a referendum victory for *Remain* instead of Leave, but again by 52–48%. Leave campaigners, drawing attention to the *closeness of the result*, call on the government to withdraw from the European Union anyway. They argue that many British people did not understand the full complexity of what they had voted about, and had been misled by the Remain campaign on several points. A critical mass of MPs begin to pursue Brexit in Parliament. The speaker of the House of Commons is suspected of supporting the Leavers and of cavalierly interpreting parliamentary procedure in ways that assist their cause. Protesters march on London to call for a second vote aimed at reversing the conclusion of the first one. Several Cabinet members declare themselves committed to making Brexit happen. In due course, political analysts begin to conclude that Brexit has indeed become a distinct possibility.

It seems hard to imagine such an alternative reality playing out all that smoothly. In fact, it seems hard to imagine it playing out without causing widespread apoplexy among people who had voted Remain, perhaps engendering a campaign of civil disobedience, if not ultimately sedition. Remainers would surely be a lot less sanguine about overturning referendum results had they won, instead of lost, the 2016 vote.

Perspective determines everything.

The failure of each side to consider the other's perspective presents a recurring irony: partisan complaints routinely mirror each other.

For example, both sides regularly accuse the other of deception. The Remain side is said to have misled the public with Project Fear, and its warnings about the immediate economic consequences of Brexit. Meanwhile, as we saw in Chapter 2, the Leave side was accused of lying about the £350 million mentioned on the side of that famous red bus.

Likewise, both sides accuse the other of breaking the rules of financial fair play. The Leave campaign was criticised for spending £500,000 more than its legal limit of £7 million (Elgot, 2018). On the other hand, the Remain campaign was criticised for appropriating £9 million of taxpayers' money to fund a leafleting blitz, despite the reality that many (if not most) taxpayers were far from supportive of the Remain cause (Stewart & Mason, 2016).

A more complex mirror-image criticism relates to xenophobia. Commentators on the Remain side have frequently suggested that Brexit garners crucial support from xenophobes and racists. As we will discuss below, there is little doubt that the Brexit furore has been seized upon by bigots, and that this dynamic has produced some extremely disturbing consequences.

However, many Leave voters are especially hurt by the accusation that they are racially intolerant. In their view, it is the European Union that is structurally xenophobic (Harris, 2019). They argue that the EU preserves freedom of movement for predominantly white Europeans, while sending gunboats into the Mediterranean to intercept, and turn away, economic migrants from the world's poorer (and less white) nations. These critics object to the European Union precisely because it operates as a culturally protectionist fiefdom.

This is not to say that all Leavers and Remainers see Brexit in identical terms, and that each side's view is precisely the opposite of the other's. Nor is it implied that everybody is right because nobody is wrong. It is to say that the divide between the Brexit tribes is as much about group dynamics as it is about morality or evidence. We know from psychological research that groups tend to polarise in ways that accentuate self-aggrandisement at the expense of the third-person effect.

Each group considers itself competent and their adversaries contemptuous. In reality, both overlook the weaknesses in their own positions, and overplay their hand when it comes to dishing out criticism. This is the natural shape of group relations as determined by human psychology.

It is one of the most important lessons we can draw from the psychology of Brexit.

Return to Psychodrama

In Chapter 1, we considered the idea that Brexit is a symptom of the United Kingdom's post-imperial demise. Such psychodrama offers a seductive story, but one that wilts under the heat of scientific scrutiny. It ignores the role of serendipity in events, is skewed by easily remembered but non-significant factoids, and fails to take account of counterexamples. Ultimately, it over-elaborates: the theory can be logically superseded by simpler explanations. Post-imperial psychodrama is a seductive rationalisation for Brexit, but not a real reason for it.

But what do we mean when we say that a narrative is 'seductive'? In essence, we mean more than just that it is widely believed. We mean that people find the narrative gratifying, that it feeds a desire that would otherwise leave them mentally hungry. It addresses their discomfort with ambiguity while endorsing their belief in human control over events. It fits explanatory gaps with a satisfying click.

This desire for an explanation—and the corresponding frustration at not having one—is sometimes referred to as a need for 'cognitive closure' (Kruglanski & Webster, 1996). It relates to the in-built human scepticism toward uncertainty, where our pattern-detecting brains assume we live in a world in which everything can be explained. It involves 'teleologic thinking', where events are overly attributed to unseen causes (Wagner-Egger, Delouvée, Gauvrit, & Dieguez, 2018).

It is why many people come to believe in conspiracies. They are attracted by claims that events are somehow driven and controlled, rather than meandering and sporadic (Marchlewska, Cichocka, & Kossowska, 2018). If you wish, therefore, the Brexit psychodrama could be seen as a type of conspiracy theory.

Conspiracy theories require a belief that the true causes of events are invisible. Usually, these causes involve shadowy factions that operate with ulterior motives. The Brexit psychodrama is a type of conspiracy theory in that it suggests that people's campaigning and voting behaviour in 2016 did not result from the causes we assume. They did not stem from people's political attitudes toward the European Union. Nor were they the result of political chaos.

Instead, Brexit is said to have transpired from hidden emotional forces rooted in the collective mental anguish of imperial decline. The underlying motivations of the people who made Brexit happen were not all that they first appeared.

Another version of teleologic thinking involves the use of nostalgia. Politicians often employ nostalgia to frame their positions on current events. The message is that history is an active force that determines how things happen today, the unseen cause that is really driving things. It also implies that Britain can look to its past for inspiration, in order to re-live its finest hours once again.

Both Leavers and Remainers have sought to invoke World War II as a guide for navigating Brexit. For Leavers, the war showed how Britain can stand alone against totalitarianism and endure. To Remainers, the war was a multinational effort that led directly to the creation of today's European Union, stimulated by Churchill's call in 1946 for 'the re-creation of the European family' and 'a United States of Europe' (Peel, 2016).

Even with nostalgia, perspective matters.

Teleologic thinking about the role of empires and past wars in shaping today's events are not the only Brexit conspiracy theories. More orthodox conspiracy theories also exist, in which secretive and malevolent agents perpetrate outright subterfuge. Once again, Brexit polarisation produces mirror-image forms of this tribal propaganda warfare.

The Leave side is convinced that a Machiavellian establishment is working to coax the political system into betraying ordinary citizens by thwarting Brexit (Pearson, 2018). Meanwhile, on the Remain side, Brexit is said to have been brought about by a 'shadowy global operation' who employed psychological techniques in order to 'influence the result' of the EU referendum (Cadwalladr, 2017).

During the 2019 European elections, there was also considerable speculation that anti-Brexit milkshake attacks on prominent Leave campaigners were in fact staged by Leavers themselves, in order to garner sympathy for their cause while casting Remainers in a negative light (Hawker, 2019). In this way, Leavers were said to be throwing milkshakes at each other as part of a 'false flag' operation, emulating the tactics of deep-state operatives or terrorist groups such as Isis.

Psychologists have found that conspiracy theories are more widely believed by people who feel politically powerless (Jolley & Douglas, 2014). They thrive in groups that hold exaggeratedly positive views of themselves (Cichocka, Marchlewska, Golec de Zavala, & Olechowski, 2016). And they are more likely to emerge in communities who feel that their future prospects are poor (Bilewicz, Winiewski, Kofta, & Wójcik, 2013). As we have seen in previous chapters, all these factors loom large in the Brexit landscape.

Not just Britain

The Brexit landscape does not solely consist of Britain. Brexit may be an episode of British destiny, but it is fundamentally an international event. One of its most complex aspects concerns the impact on Northern Ireland, the part of the United Kingdom that shares a land border with the Republic of Ireland and thus with the EU.

The future economic impact of Brexit on Northern Ireland is difficult to predict, insofar as much depends on the exact terms under which the UK eventually leaves the European Union. The cultural impact is also complicated.

Currently, under the Good Friday Agreement, citizens of Northern Ireland are automatically entitled to birthright citizenship of the Republic of Ireland. As such, they are entitled to hold European Union citizenship too. Once the UK withdraws from the European Union, how the relationship between these citizens and the EU will operate is currently unclear. As we saw in Chapter 4, lack of clarity is a situational risk factor for psychological stress.

More tangibly, there is also the issue of the international border that lies between Northern Ireland and the Republic. In reality this border is primarily a cartographical concept, existing only on maps.

The establishment of the European Single Market in 1993 saw the ending of tax restrictions and tariffs between the UK and the Republic of Ireland, permitting free travel of goods and services between the two countries. After the Northern Ireland peace process took hold in the late 1990s, security infrastructure was removed, a burgeoning cross-border trade emerged, and ultimately daily life in nearby communities blended into a single shared existence.

The border is 310 miles long but is intersected by nearly 300 crossing points. As well as motorways and roads, there are country lanes, private roads, rights of way on private lands, and similar traditional access routes. In 2018, the Irish army completed a mapping exercise that revealed significantly more cross-border traffic routes than had previously been included on official maps (Sheehan, 2018).

In some instances, next-door neighbours live on adjoining farms either side of the border. In other cases, a single farm can straddle both sides. The farmer makes a daily choice whether to tend the herd of cattle next to the farmhouse in the Republic, or the other one across the yard in the United Kingdom (Murtagh, 2019).

Whatever form it takes, Brexit will inevitably complicate life for people who live and work near the border. Some forms of Brexit would require security checkpoints to ensure that goods crossing from one country to the other are appropriately certified. Given the extensively agricultural economy, where short-range transport of fresh food produce makes up the bulk of trade, the economic impact of costly export tariffs and transport delays would be extremely severe.

There is also an eventual prospect that personal papers would need to be scrutinised, to ensure that people who cross the border are visa-compliant. Quite how all this would operate in the many cases where the border cuts through private property is unclear.

Of greatest concern is the relationship between EU membership and the Northern Ireland peace process. This process, culminating in the Good Friday Agreement of 1998, effectively brought an end to a bitter conflict that had taken the lives of over 3500 victims across a thirty-year period. The fact that both Britain and Ireland were member states of the European Union provided a cultural backdrop to peace, in that it facilitated complete freedom of movement and trade across the border, as well as interchangeable citizenship status.

Peace in Northern Ireland is widely understood to be an ongoing work in progress. There continues to be violence, although at a greatly reduced level. Around one hundred and fifty people have been killed in dissident paramilitary activities since the Good Friday Agreement was signed.

The fear that Brexit could precipitate a return to full-scale conflict stems from the fact that it would undermine cross-border cooperation, deplete EU funding for post-conflict restoration, damage the economy, and reinstate the type of formal political partition that so aggravated inter-community tensions in the past.

Mental illness and suicide in Northern Ireland are already higher than in other regions of the UK, with research suggesting that the excess relates to the decades of political violence (Ferry et al., 2013). In contrast, the peace process has provided hope for an economically and socially prosperous future, and has given many people meaning for their suffering (O'Neill, 2019).

Should Brexit result in a denigration, or collapse, of the Northern Ireland peace process, it will inevitably threaten the welfare of an already vulnerable population.

The Irish Question(s)

South of the border in Ireland, perspectives on Brexit skew mostly negative, for a variety of economic, social, and cultural reasons. The economy, in particular, is severely threatened.

Trade barriers with the United Kingdom would transform life for Irish food producers, much of whose business relies on just-in-time delivery to British supermarkets. Industries that export further afield would also be affected, as Britain is essentially Ireland's land bridge to Europe. Goods are typically transported by truck, through the United Kingdom.

Brexit will create intense pressure on the Irish economy. The extra costs of managing increasingly complex export logistics, the levying of tariffs that would make Irish produce immediately more expensive in Britain, and delays in transport that would render perishable food unsellable, create extremely threatening practicalities for the Republic of Ireland.

Any post-Brexit recession in Ireland can be expected to result in exactly the same type of mental health impact that we discussed in Chapter 4.

Unsurprisingly, the Irish media are very focused on Brexit. An Oxford University analysis of European news reporting found that while most European countries discuss Brexit as a problem for the UK, in Ireland it is considered an Irish crisis as much as it is a British one (Borchardt, Bironzo, & Simon, 2018).

To date, few formal psychological studies of the Irish perspective on Brexit have been conducted. Media reporting suggests that, for most Irish people, anxiety over the economy and the peace process is coupled with sympathy for British neighbours living very much in the eye of the Brexit storm.

There is, however, fear about the British political attitude towards Ireland. Statements by UK politicians that reveal naiveté regarding Ireland's economic and political realities are extensively reported (Ní Aodha, 2018). According to some commentators, this anxiety feeds into a broader sense of *schadenfreude* among many Irish people, who complacently scoff at Britain's apparent willingness to 'self-destruct' (Mac Cormaic, 2018).

The psychology of group dynamics is just as relevant to international relations as it is to Brexit's internecine tribal conflicts. The perils of strong in-group identification, the desire for optimal distinctiveness, and the biases of out-group homogeneity all play their part. It can be useful to consider the Irish perspective on Brexit with them in mind.

For example, in Chapter 2, we examined the widespread claim that Brexit amounts to a form of 'economic self-harm'. The day after the referendum, the *Irish Times* was one of the first international newspapers to describe Brexit in such terms. Its editorial announced that Ireland's British neighbours had just performed an 'act of self-harm' that was 'bewildering' in its scale and impact:

> The truth is that the shocking decision of the UK to leave the European Union, genuinely bewildering to its friends and allies across the Irish Sea and the continent, will leave the kingdom neither independent nor united. It will be poorer, more isolated and less influential. Our neighbours have inflicted a deep wound on their country, economically and politically. (Irish Times, 2016)

However, Irish history itself provides a thought-provoking parallel to the Brexit experience.

In essence, Brexit involves a country wilfully choosing to extricate itself from a pan-national consortium with a population of 500 million. It has chosen to separate for largely nationalistic reasons, and is willing to take whatever economic risk such a step might involve. In a number of ways, this resembles the departure of Ireland from the UK itself in 1922, and in due course from the British Empire as a whole.

Just like with Brexit, in 1922 Ireland was choosing to withdraw from a hugely influential pan-national entity. The British Empire at that time also had a population of around 500 million inhabitants. Ireland was willing to take the economic hit of leaving the UK, because it wished to prioritise its right to national self-determination (in fact, echoing Project Fear, Irish politicians at the time argued that their country would suffer economically should it *remain* within the UK). Another relevant narrative was Ireland's desire to distance itself from the imperial militarism of the British superstructure.

Most Irish people look back on their country's exit from the United Kingdom in romantic nationalist terms. Parallels with Brexit are rarely mentioned. Nationalism, self-determination, and liberty are considered entirely justifiable reasons for Ireland to have taken its economic leap-in-the-dark in 1922. Irish independence is seldom decried as having been a bewildering act of economic self-harm.

As such, perhaps these same motivations should be acknowledged as legitimate reasons for Leavers to invoke in support of Brexit today. Once more, perspective matters. Rather than cultivating self-comforting *schadenfreude*, the Irish historical perspective could potentially be mined for insights that help elucidate the modern psychology of Brexit.

'Why Haven't They Left Yet?'

A final set of Brexit perspectives relates to the inherently multicultural nature of British society. As we saw in Chapter 3, the United Kingdom's four constituent countries each seem to be characterised by different Brexit opinions. Moreover, citizens' personal national identities—such as whether they identify as 'English', 'Scottish', or 'British'—have been shown to predict their feelings about Brexit.

But beyond these broad country-level identities, the UK also enjoys a great deal of cultural and ethnic diversity. Approximately one-in-eight of the population are of non-white ethnicity. Fourteen per cent of the population were born outside the UK. Of these, around a third—some 3.7 million people—were born in other European Union countries. This latter group are faced with considerable uncertainty regarding Brexit, because their entitlement to live in the UK is premised on Britain's EU membership.

Even in the most stable times, members of ethnic minority groups are at elevated risk of mental health difficulties (Bhugra, 2005). Since the Brexit referendum, a number of minority groups have experienced additional stress.

Migrants from EU countries have received no clarification of their likely post-Brexit immigration status. They do not know if they can continue to be employed in the UK without a visa, or if they will be deported. Advocacy groups representing these migrants report that many are burdened with extreme anxiety and other mental health problems (Bueltmann, 2019).

Meanwhile, members of ethnic minorities have found themselves increasingly targeted by racial and ethnic harassment. It is one of the most disturbing realities of Brexit that anti-immigration campaigners have seized the opportunity to conflate British isolationism with an ambiguous form of monoculturalism. British racism has once again been allowed to rear its ugly head.

During the referendum campaign, some pro-Leave campaigners pursued particularly controversial anti-immigrant strategies. One effect was to create a generalised increase in tolerance for racist language. As one economics journalist put it: 'After a campaign scarred by bigotry, it's become OK to be racist in Britain' (Chakrabortty, 2016).

In the aftermath of Britain voting to leave the European Union, there was a sharp and sudden increase in reports of racist incidents. Multiple anti-racism organisations described being swamped by calls and messages (Khaleeli, 2016).

A number of ethnic minority businesses were firebombed, homes were graffitied, and in several towns cards reading 'No more Polish vermin', in both English and Polish, were posted through letterboxes (Lyons, 2016). There were many reports of people being harassed on the street, jeered at in shops, and barracked at passport control in airports. One sociologist described the reaction as the unleashing of 'celebratory racism' (Ridley, 2016). Survey data suggest that these increases in racial hostility have been maintained in the three years since the referendum (Booth, 2019).

Racial and ethnic discrimination is not just a social ill, it is also a chronic stressor that is known to increase the risk of mental illness and poor physical health (Bhui, 2016). Data from the UK Household Longitudinal Study show that exposure to racial discrimination in Britain is associated with cumulative mental ill-health across time (Wallace, Nazroo, & Bécares, 2016). In other words, if you encounter racism, your mental health will suffer; and if you encounter racism repeatedly, your mental health will suffer more.

Withdrawal from the European Union will create complications for immigrants from EU countries, as well as disruption to cross-border trade. But Brexit has no particular bearing on naturalised citizens, immigrants from non-EU countries, or minority religious groups. Nonetheless, Brexit tensions have often involved hostility against *all* non-indigenous cultural minorities, including those where there is no particular EU dimension (Heald, Vida, Farman, & Bhugra, 2018).

A recurring example is British Muslims (Jackson, 2017). When the anti-racism group Hope Not Hate conducted door-to-door research in Bradford after the Brexit referendum, they observed a marked increase in the open expression of wide-ranging racist views tied explicitly to Brexit. According to one of their researchers, this included 'white people pointing at the Asian family down the road, saying: "*Why haven't they left yet?*"' (Williams, 2019).

As a project of political disruption, Brexit has drawn the attention of the type of nationalist-populist movements that have been on the rise across Europe and globally. Undoubtedly such disruption is an after-effect of economic recession and austerity.

It is often easier to direct public anger toward visible targets, such as immigrants, than against an abstract political programme or economic policy (Cromby, 2019). As we saw in Chapter 1, human beings engage in various rationalisation processes to make sense of their discomforts. One of the most powerful, and ancient, of these strategies is scapegoating.

The group polarisation at the centre of Brexit is, of course, two-sided. Reported increases in racist incidents reflects one pole of society. At the other pole, by contrast, has been a gradual increase of expressed *support* for the concept of immigration in Britain.

Data from the British Election Study show that positive views about the economic and cultural impacts of immigration have increased steadily since 2016 (Blinder & Richards, 2018). The number of respondents to the British Social Attitudes survey who want to strengthen controls on EU migrants has significantly decreased during the same period (Harding, 2017). And the number of voters telling Ipsos-MORI that that immigration is an 'important problem' has halved, and is now at its lowest level since 2001 (Ipsos MORI, 2017).

The United Kingdom is diverse not just culturally and ethnically. It is also diverse in the way it perceives, experiences, and reacts to life. It is diverse psychologically.

That range of human conditions is one of the reasons why the psychology of Brexit is such an important issue. One size does not fit all. Neither do two sizes: Leaver and Remainer. Instead, there are a myriad of different perspectives—an abundance of perceptions and experiences to consider.

II. Ten Lessons from the Psychology of Brexit

Brexit is psychological in its causes, catalysts, and consequences. The psychology of Brexit provides us with many insights, and many lessons to learn. Let us conclude this journey through the psychology of Brexit by considering them in turn.

Lesson 1: Ignore the Psychodrama, but Learn from History

In many ways, history resembles psychology. It tries to provide explanations for human experiences. But in some ways, history itself is an offshoot of psychological forces. For reasons to do with emotion, self-regard, social influence, and selective memory, people are often inclined towards some historical explanations more than others.

As we discussed above, nostalgia allows history to be used for political gain. Nostalgia is a deliberately subjective form of history, skewed by the rose-tinted glasses that we considered in Chapter 2. The *Sunday Times* journalist AA Gill memorably warned about its use in Brexit debates:

> We all know what 'getting our country back' means. It's snorting a line of the most pernicious and debilitating Little English drug, nostalgia. The warm, crumbly, honey-coloured, collective 'yesterday' with its fond belief that everything was better back then, that Britain (England, really) is a worse place now than it was at some foggy point in the past where we achieved peak Blighty. (Gill, 2016)

In some ways, history as a whole is susceptible to a nostalgic psychology. Adept historians often warn against a story-telling approach that depicts historical events as a saga of continuous human improvement (Watson, 2019). Things do not necessarily get better with the passing of time.

The risks we face today are not qualitatively different from those that faced our ancestors. Sudden economic shock coupled with rising populism and blithe self-aggrandising optimism have, in the past, led to global war.

The problem is that, psychologically, we cannot remember the past except through historical distortion. It is useful to learn from psychology that whenever we consider ourselves more cautious than our predecessors, more sophisticated in our behaviours, and less likely to repeat their mistakes, these beliefs are in fact delusions. We should not assume that yesterday's tragedies can never occur again.

As we discussed in Chapter 1, there is more to history than diplomacy and politics. Social life and intellectual ideas from the past are also relevant. It is also important to take a scientific approach to these things. The best historical explanations are ones that are evidence-based and tested against counter-examples.

When it comes to politics, it is understandable that commentators look to the past in order to interpret current events. It is understandable, for example, that people consider Brexit in terms of post-imperial psychodrama. However, the use of history to account for the thoughts, feelings, and behaviours of people living today is not straightforward. Rhetorical history is no substitute for methodical psychology. In learning from the past, we need to allow for the self-serving biases that intrude on our efforts to 'do' history, and not be lulled by seductive nostalgic narratives.

Lesson 2: Mental Autonomy Is a Tempting and Consoling Bias—People Are More Influenced by Situational Factors and Consensus Than They Realise

As pointed out in Chapter 2, human beings are not quite as rational as they think they are. Rather than work out the logical solution to a problem, people will instead take mental shortcuts on the road to their conclusions.

They weigh information not for its merit, but on the basis of how easily it is remembered. They are swayed by first impressions and trivial details. And they attach undue importance to whatever they can personally relate to themselves.

Layered on all this is the mental choreography of social relations. Humans can become very convinced by points other people have made, simply on the basis that they have made them. This is true even if those points objectively make no sense. The compulsion to save face leads people to breezily agree with statements they do not understand. Common knowledge more often reflects shared delusion than useful consensus.

An important consequence is that few people react positively when they are told they have got everything wrong. In political debate, myth-busting might be satisfying for the myth-buster, but the strategy changes relatively few minds. Telling your audience they have been duped is akin to telling them they are stupid. They are more likely to cling to their prior ideas than believe themselves to be fools when these ideas are challenged.

And incidentally, so too are you. Your Brexit positions are more influenced by situational factors and consensus than you realise. And you stick to your guns with disproportionate vigour when they are criticised.

The psychology of Brexit shows us that when it comes to formulating and defending a political position, all of us combine overconfidence with underperformance. We entirely underestimate the extent to which we are influenced by irrelevant details, false assumptions, and the things other people say.

Lesson 3: The 'Will of the People' Has Poor Construct Validity

In psychology, most of our research is centred on the task of measurement. We are always looking for ways to accurately calibrate emotions, thoughts, personality traits, attitudes, abilities, preferences, and so on. This is easier said than done. Psychology is a science, yes, but measuring intelligence, anger, or happiness is a lot harder than measuring time, distance, or weight.

The use of a referendum to gauge opinion is effectively psychological research. With Brexit, the objective was to measure whether the British people wanted their country to withdraw from the European Union. The voting paper was essentially a questionnaire. The sample size was in excess of thirty million. The result of the referendum—Leave—was the measurement.

And the margin of error? Well, we don't know what that was.

Which is a pity, because all psychological measurement has a margin of error. If you ever did an IQ test, you would have found that as well as a score, your result will have included a range. For many people, their IQ will be, say, 100 *plus or minus 5*. For the sake of accuracy, that margin of error is crucial. Precision and correctness are not always the same thing. In fact, precision is often the enemy of correctness.

When a psychological measurement is correct, we say that it has 'construct validity'. This means that the measurement is a true depiction of the reality that is being measured.

An IQ score has construct validity if it provides a true reflection of a person's intelligence. A happiness score will have construct validity if it tells us how happy they are. Much comes down to defining what you are looking for in terms that are clear, precise, and accurate. As you might imagine, in psychology, construct validity is hard.

Many commentators discuss the Brexit result as representing the 'will of the people.' However, as we saw in Chapter 3, the people do not possess a single will. As such, referring to the will of the people is an example of the ecological fallacy. It involves presuming a generality where there is, in fact, variety. It has poor construct validity.

When a psychology research study is found to have poor construct validity, it is considered essentially worthless. However, you can often learn something by picking through the bones of the results, if only to try to figure out what it was your study died of.

As such, the Brexit result can indeed be interpreted and acted upon intelligently. However, its outcome requires detailed consideration and cautious interpretation. Depicting the result as a singular 'will of the people' is self-evidently erroneous. Claiming to 'respect' this will, while simultaneously misrepresenting it, is nothing less than a contradiction in terms.

The challenge of construct validity should not be taken lightly. Unless the challenge is met, the Brexit impasse will not easily be resolved by any second referendum, never mind a general election. Direct democracy sounds like a good idea in principle, but it is extremely hard to perfect in real life.

Lesson 4: People Make Partisan Decisions, but Systematically Overestimate Their Own Logic and Soundness

Not only do human beings make irrational decisions that are influenced by situational factors, they also systematically fail to notice the flaws in their own views. Meanwhile, they obsessively presume any contrary argument to be full of holes.

We saw in Chapter 2 how out-group homogeneity bias causes Leavers and Remainers to hold themselves in high esteem but to look down on each other. And because of the third-person effect, both Brexit tribes consider themselves resistant to delusion, while believing their adversaries to be deluded beyond rescue.

As we saw earlier in this chapter, one of the biggest psychological challenges of Brexit is the difficulty people face in considering perspectives other than their own. We are naturally loyal to our own opinions. Our social, self-preserving, pattern-detecting brains have evolved to make hypocrites of us all. We hold other people, other *tribes*, to a higher standard than we apply to ourselves.

This bias makes us susceptible to political rhetoric. Simple phrases are often all it takes to convince us of our own correctness. It is easy to get excited about 'taking back control' when we ignore the fact that other countries might want to take some control too (Rogers, 2019). By playing on people's natural proneness to agree with themselves, political rhetoric does more to excite than to convince.

Forcing yourself to see the other side's perspective is very difficult. It is unnatural. However, to resolve political disputes such as Brexit, as difficult and as unnatural as it is, it is also absolutely necessary.

Lesson 5: Everything Is Social

As we saw in Chapter 3, even the most isolationist, introverted, or anti-social person is, in fact, part of a communitarian species. You cannot even think your own thoughts without using a language that you only ever learned in order to communicate with others. There would be no Brexit without other people. Brexit is enmeshed in a sea of relationships, reciprocities, and social identities.

The ability to be free and independent is itself a social status. The United Kingdom holds regular open elections and benefits from a vibrant media. It is one of the world's most democratic countries. In global and historic terms, British people are among the freest who have ever lived.

Psychologically, this can sometimes encourage people toward disruptive, rather than cohesive, action. For some people, the sign of a true democracy—and perhaps the only *reliable* sign—is being able to do something that everyone is telling you should not be done.

For many people Brexit is a rebellion against being told what to do all the time, a culture war in which a long marginalised out-group finally gets to take over. Britons, they believe, never, never, never shall be slaves.

In one episode of the British sitcom *Peep Show*, lead character Jeremy contemplates whether or not he should kiss his roommate's crush. 'This is almost definitely a terrible idea,' his internal monologue tells him, 'but I won't know for certain until I've actually done it' (Armstrong & Bain, 2007). Sometimes, disruption of the status quo is the only way of testing just how free you actually are.

This is one of the reasons people become rigidly fixed in their Brexit positions when challenged. As discussed in Chapter 2, identity-protective motivated reasoning can produce a backfire effect. Being attacked or ridiculed often makes people *more*, rather than less, committed to their views. They intensely resist the attempt by other people to constrain their freedom of choice.

Lesson 6: Groups Descend Quickly into Vicious Cycles of Polarisation

One of the most striking features of Brexit is its divisiveness. In a relatively short period of time, an entire society has become dichotomised. And as time passes, the two Brexit tribes drift further apart. This is propelled by the problems of perspective we discussed above. It is compounded by confirmation bias, asymmetric feedback, and communicating within echo chambers (analogue as well as digital).

In general, relationships grow slowly but fall apart quickly. Integration is often a detailed effort, where a steady pace is required to keep all objectives in view. Disintegration, by contrast, is chaotic. Its pace is accelerated. A relationship, when damaged, may never fully recover. In the history of human culture, schisms often last centuries.

The binary nature of group polarisation is itself artificial. In reality, even though there are two main tribes, Leaver and Remainer, there are many different views on Brexit within each. As we discussed in Chapter 3, to pursue a two-tribe approach is itself to flirt with the ecological fallacy.

Not only are Leavers and Remainers internally diverse, so too are Britain and the European Union. Many people in Britain disagree about what would constitute a good deal with the EU, but British negotiators must present a single UK position. The EU side, representing twenty-seven national governments, must also grapple with multiple viewpoints. This all makes any Brexit talks particularly complicated. As argued by negotiations expert and psychologist Thomas Hills:

> Imagine buying a car and giving all your friends and relatives the right to veto your choice. Now imagine that you also give the same power to all the car dealerships you visit. That's Brexit. (Hills, 2019)

Effective collaboration requires bringing people together in a way that promotes mutual perspective-taking and self-criticism. Groups polarise naturally. The problem takes effort to avoid or undo.

Lesson 7: When Game Theory Ensures that Everybody Loses, Stop Playing

In Chapter 3, we saw how Leavers and Remainers are involved in an arms-race dynamic in parliament. Neither side will agree to collaborate with the other in order to reduce risk. Because of the game theory logic of the prisoner's dilemma, the only end-point is impasse. The options are straightforward. It is *No Deal or No Deal.*

Such logjams result from poor reasoning, irreconcilable tensions, and toxic relationships. The dynamic has made it virtually impossible for a withdrawal agreement to be passed by parliament. The natural ending is that the system crashes. Either the United Kingdom leaves the European Union with no deal, or a general election is called and its government is rebooted at the ballot box. Or perhaps both: switching the UK off and back on again might not fix the problem.

One psychologically interesting way to deal with such quagmires was employed by the ancient Athenians to choose their leaders. It was called 'sortition'. In plainer language, it means a lottery. You draw your options out of a hat.

The Greeks recognised that certain types of votes encouraged politicians to issue undeliverable promises, to make unsupportable assertions, and to disagree with their rivals simply in order to differentiate themselves. All of these bad habits were neutralised by using sortition, instead of voting, to choose between options.

Selecting the outcome at random served to sanitise decisions. It prevented grudges between winners and losers that might contaminate future group dynamics. Nobody can be envied for being pandered to when a decision is taken at random. And nobody can be blamed for their error afterwards, should things not work out.

Sortition was an early recognition that humans overestimate their own ability to reason through problems. Some challenges are just too complicated. The illusion of control is just that, an illusion. A decision based on no reason at all seems preferable to one that might be based on poor reasons.

Such a lottery can be recommended where decision-makers have already screened out bad ideas and have arrived at a fixed number of remaining options. One psychology professor at the University of Warwick has argued that the UK has achieved this in its Brexit negotiations (Liu, 2019). The Brexit deadlock in parliament might be resolved if MPs were to agree to roll a dice or toss a coin.

Based on the psychology of group polarisation, rose-tinted glasses, and the incorrigibility of bias, a Brexit lottery might not necessarily be all that absurd.

Lesson 8: A Conscientious Administration Will Prepare for Mental Health Consequences

In Chapter 4, we saw how Brexit is contributing to significant anxiety in large segments of the population. Opinion polls consistently reveal that people find Brexit stressful, and that it interferes with their daily well-being and relationships. Objective empirical research has corroborated what the opinion pollsters have been saying. It also reveals the stress of Brexit to be getting worse rather than better.

A wider research literature conclusively demonstrates that economic and political uncertainty poses risks to mental health. Recession, joblessness, and social deprivation each contribute to severe pathology. The research evidence is clear and consistent. Increases in unemployment lead to increases in suicide.

Some people in the United Kingdom are more vulnerable than others. People in Northern Ireland face the additional stress of a precarious peace process. Members of ethnic minorities find themselves targeted by racist harassment.

As pointed out in Chapter 4, there is nothing inherently traumatic in Britain exiting the European Union. All the danger comes from how the process is managed. Nations are entitled to exercise their autonomy in ways that risk economic recession. The important thing is that they do so with appropriate preparation.

In dealing with Brexit, a conscientious government should invest in services that provide targeted support to vulnerable groups. It should prepare for recession by augmenting mental health services, and make focused efforts to address the specific spike in suicide that all the research tells us will inevitably result. A conscientious electorate should hold their government to account should it fail to protect citizens in this way.

Lesson 9: A Conscientious Administration Will Go to Effort to Reduce Situational Risk Factors

It is argued in Chapter 4 that Brexit is a case study in how to steer a major national project in the most stressful way possible. This is because of the actions of politicians and public administrators. They have dealt with Brexit in ways that have exacerbated the problems of ambiguity, role vagueness, low control, poverty of feedback, inconsistency of reward, interpersonal conflict, low social support, and unpredictability. All of these are known situational risk factors for stress.

Brexit has caused nationwide upheaval in the UK. It has shattered norms of daily life that people had become accustomed to in previous decades. In that sense, Brexit has the feel of a real national emergency. Some might even call it a disaster.

Brexit is not a flood or earthquake or fire, nor is it a war or terrorist attack. However, it is an interminable day-to-day stressor that has implications for just about everybody who lives in the United Kingdom. As low-level catastrophes go, its reach is far more extensive than most. Likewise, Brexit is likely to last much longer than most upheavals. Its social and economic implications will persist for generations.

Psychologists who study catastrophes have long noted that human beings are surprisingly resilient. People frequently spring into action in ways that show solidarity in the face of trauma (Kaniasty & Norris, 2004). However, natural disasters are different to those created by human hands. In a human-made disaster, the sense of community solidarity is often tainted. This undermines people's resilience and hampers their ability to cope (Kaniasty & Norris, 2009).

At least a human-made crisis offers the possibility that it might one day be *un*made by humans. There is a sense that human control can be established over events. Convincing citizens that things are under control would certainly do a lot to reduce the stressfulness of Brexit.

Governments and public officials have the capacity to provide better clarity. They can provide better feedback, give people a sense of purpose to voting, and display visible efforts to avoid, rather than exploit, conflict. Insofar as the situational stress factors of the Brexit crisis are controllable, conscientious leaders should surely do everything they can to take back such control.

Lesson 10: Brexit Is Psychological, Not Political

Throughout this book one thing has been clear: Brexit is profoundly psychological. In Chapter 1, we saw how Brexit provokes widespread efforts to explain political upheaval by invoking deeply embedded cultural concepts that penetrate the British psyche. In Chapter 2, we examined the impact of evolved human decision-making brains on perceptions and experiences of Brexit.

In Chapter 3, we saw how Brexit reflects the way individual British citizens psychologically experience their lives, how they identify themselves culturally, and what values they hold. And in Chapter 4, we reflected on the impact of Brexit on a population's mental well-being, as well as the way that population judges their own sanity through the lens of Brexit hindsight.

Brexit is all about feelings, assumptions, influences, dispositions, social relations, identities, emotions, pathologies, and perspectives. Brexit is indeed profoundly psychological.

Of course the politics, economics, and logistics of Brexit all warrant close attention. And Brexit will keep historians, geographers, and sociologists busy for decades. To say that Brexit is psychological and not political is to emphasise its emotional and behavioural aspects. Politics itself is a fundamentally psychological activity.

Politics is about understanding what people what, how they feel, and what they believe. Politicians cannot function if they cannot judge what is in people's minds, not least their own. Politics is enhanced when we understand how human beings make choices, what motivates them, and where their potential lies.

Dealing with Brexit by focusing on customs unions, trade, regulations, and red-tape is necessary to an extent. But there is also a sense in which technocracy serves as a distraction. It is much easier to count beans than to fulfil ambitions, navigate ethics, or inspire nations. And it is easier to go through the political motions than to heal communities, to address dire needs, or to build better futures.

The resolution of Brexit needs to account for people's personalities, their emotions, and their sense of place in the world. Psychology is a science, but science can often reduce to its own type of bean-counting. The wonders of psychology are its insights into the pure souls of people, its capacity to achieve emotional communion, and the mental periscope it offers, through which we can view ourselves, and our assumptions, from different angles.

The psychology of Brexit is important, therefore, not only because it helps us to appreciate Brexit. It also helps us to appreciate the idea of humans having a 'psychology' per se. We can use Brexit to explain psychology, as we use psychology to examine Brexit. And from this we can better recognise our own selves, our proclivities and weaknesses, our potential and well-being.

Brexit is psychological, not political. It is a finite experience, an episode of mental life, the outflow of a series of behavioural actions and mental endeavours, by individuals and societies. It is one of the most profound social upheavals that we will witness in our lifetimes. It can, and should, be studied.

Brexit is Brexit. And we should all seek to learn from it.

References

Ahmad, F., Jhajj, A. K., Stewart, D. E., Burghardt, M., & Bierman, A. S. (2014). Single item measures of self-rated mental health: A scoping review. *BMC Health Services Research, 14,* 398.

Altemeyer, B. (1998). The other 'authoritarian personality'. *Advances in Experimental Social Psychology, 30,* 47–92.

American Psychological Association. (1992, April 1). *Guidelines for nonhandicapping language in APA journals.* Retrieved from https://apastyle.apa.org/manual/related/nonhandicapping-language.html.

American Psychological Association. (2010). *Publication manual of the American Psychological Association* (6th ed.). Washington, DC: APA.

Armstrong, J., & Bain, S. (2007). *Peep Show s04e02: 'Conference'.* Retrieved from https://www.imdb.com/title/tt1017808/fullcredits.

Arvey, R. D., Rotundo, M., Johnson, W., Zhang, Z., & McGue, M. (2006). The determinants of leadership role occupancy: Genetic and personality factors. *Leadership Quarterly, 17,* 1–20.

Ashcroft, L. (2016, June 24). *How the United Kingdom voted on Thursday…and why.* Lord Ashcroft Polls. Retrieved from https://lordashcroftpolls.com/2016/06/how-the-united-kingdom-voted-and-why/.

Ashdown, P. (2017, March 29). Brexit is a monumental act of self-harm which will bewilder historians. *The Independent.* Retrieved from https://www.

independent.co.uk/voices/article-50-brexit-theresa-may-eu-negotiations-paddy-ashdown-monumental-self-harm-bewilder-historians-a7656306.html.

Ashdown, P. (2018, July 17). *We are at the point where no Brexit outcome can find a Commons majority: So what now?* HuffPost. Retrieved from: https://www.huffingtonpost.co.uk/entry/brexit-parliament_uk_5b4dea88e4b0fd5c73bf17b2.

BACP. (2019, April 11). *One third of adults say Brexit has affected their mental health, BACP research finds.* BACP. Retrieved from: https://www.bacp.co.uk/news/news-from-bacp/2019/11-april-one-third-of-adults-say-brexit-has-affected-their-mental-health-bacp-research-finds/.

Barberá, P., Jost, J. T., Nagler, J., Tucker, J. A., & Bonneau, R. (2015). Tweeting from left to right: Is online political communication more than an echo chamber? *Psychological Science, 26,* 1531–1542.

Barr, B., Taylor-Robinson, D., Scott-Samuel, A., McKee, M., & Stuckler, D. (2012). Suicides associated with the 2008–10 economic recession in England: Time trend analysis. *BMJ, 345,* e5142.

Bartlett, N. (2019, March 29). Boris Johnson and Jacob Rees-Mogg jeered as they fold and back Theresa May over Brexit. *Mirror.* Retrieved from https://www.mirror.co.uk/news/politics/boris-johnson-jacob-rees-mogg-14204582.

Bastos, M., Mercea, D., & Baronchelli, A. (2018). The geographic embedding of online echo chambers: Evidence from the Brexit campaign. *PLOS ONE, 13,* e0206841.

BBC News. (2017, January 23). *Cambridge scientists consider fake news 'vaccine'.* BBC. Retrieved from https://www.bbc.com/news/uk-38714404.

Begg, I. M., Anas, A., & Farinacci, S. (1992). Dissociation of processes in belief: Source recollection, statement familiarity, and the illusion of truth. *Journal of Experimental Psychology: General, 121,* 446–458.

Belam, M. (2017, November 14). Sex, slang, steak: Views that show remainers and leavers are worlds apart. *The Guardian.* Retrieved from https://www.theguardian.com/politics/2017/nov/14/sex-slang-steak-views-leave-remain-worlds-apart.

Beveridge, A. (2003). The madness of politics. *Journal of the Royal Society of Medicine, 96,* 602–604.

Bhugra, D. (2005). Cultural identities and cultural congruency: A new model for evaluating mental distress in immigrants. *Acta Psychiatrica Scandinavica., 111,* 84–93.

Bhui, K. (2016). Discrimination, poor mental health, and mental illness. *International Journal of Psychiatry, 28,* 411–414.

Bilewicz, M., Winiewski, M., Kofta, M., & Wójcik, A. (2013). Harmful ideas: The structure and consequences of antisemitic beliefs in Poland. *Political Psychology, 34,* 821–839.

Bishop, D. (2019, March 27). *What is driving Theresa May?* Deevybee. Retrieved from https://deevybee.blogspot.com/2019/03/what-is-driving-theresa-may.html.

Blinder, S., & Richards, L. (2018, June 7). *UK public opinion toward immigration: Overall attitudes and level of concern.* Migration Observatory. Retrieved from https://migrationobservatory.ox.ac.uk/resources/briefings/uk-public-opinion-toward-immigration-overall-attitudes-and-level-of-concern/.

Blitz, J. (2019, May 15). Why Theresa May faces defeat on her flagship Brexit bill. *Financial Times.* Retrieved from https://www.ft.com/content/9d4612ac-7719-11e9-be7d-6d846537acab.

Bonnie, R. J. (2002). Political abuse of psychiatry in the Soviet Union and in China: Complexities and controversies. *Journal of the American Academy of Psychiatry and the Law, 30,* 136–144.

Booth, R. (2019, March 6). Brexit vote brought UK feelgood factor to abrupt halt, says ONS. *The Guardian.* Retrieved from https://www.theguardian.com/politics/2019/mar/06/brexit-referendum-brought-uk-feelgood-factor-to-abrupt-halt-says-ons.

Borchardt, A., Bironzo, D., & Simon, F. M. (2018, July 3). *What bothers European media most about Brexit?* LSE. Retrieved from https://blogs.lse.ac.uk/brexit/2018/07/03/what-bothers-european-media-most-about-brexit/.

Boyle, N. (2018, January 16). Brexit is a collective English mental breakdown. *Irish Times.* Retrieved from https://www.irishtimes.com/opinion/brexit-is-a-collective-english-mental-breakdown-1.3356258.

Brooks, T. (2016, October 1). *The meaningless mantra of 'Brexit means Brexit'.* E!Sharp. Retrieved from https://esharp.eu/debates/the-uk-and-europe/the-meaningless-mantra-of-brexit-means-brexit.

Bueltmann, T. (2019, March 21). Five million EU and UK citizens have spent 1,000 days in limbo. It has to end. *The Guardian.* Retrieved from https://www.theguardian.com/commentisfree/2019/mar/21/five-million-eu-citizens-1000-days-limbo.

Busby, M. (2018, June 29). 'Where is the geezer?' Danny Dyer rages at David Cameron over Brexit. *The Guardian.* Retrieved from https://www.theguardian.com/film/2018/jun/29/where-is-the-geezer-danny-dyer-rages-at-david-cameron-over-brexit.

Butter, S. (2018, November 26). Are you suffering from Branxiety? *Evening Standard*. Retrieved from https://www.standard.co.uk/lifestyle/london-life/the-age-of-branxiety-a4000116.html.

Cadwalladr, C. (2017, May 7). The great British Brexit robbery: How our democracy was hijacked. *The Guardian*. Retrieved from https://www.theguardian.com/technology/2017/may/07/the-great-british-brexit-robbery-hijacked-democracy.

Caplan, B. (2001). Rational ignorance versus rational irrationality. *Kyklos, 54,* 3–26.

Carlyle, T. (1841). *On heroes, hero-worship, and the heroic in history.* London: James Fraser.

Carothers, B. J., & Reis, H. T. (2013). Men and women are from Earth: Examining the latent structure of gender. *Journal of Personality and Social Psychology, 104,* 385–407.

Carroll, P. (2018, December 5). *The facts may have changed on Brexit: But people's minds have not.* Ipsos MORI. Retrieved from https://www.ipsos.com/ipsos-mori/en-uk/facts-may-have-changed-brexit-peoples-minds-have-not.

Carswell, S. (2018, December 10). This means war: Psychologists try to make sense of Brexit. *Irish Times.* Retrieved from https://www.irishtimes.com/news/politics/this-means-war-psychologists-try-to-make-sense-of-brexit-1.3725395.

Chakrabortty, A. (2016, June 28). After a campaign scarred by bigotry, it's become OK to be racist in Britain. *The Guardian.* Retrieved from https://www.theguardian.com/commentisfree/2016/jun/28/campaign-bigotry-racist-britain-leave-brexit.

Chomsky, N. (1957). *Syntactic structures.* The Hague: Mouton.

Cichocka, A., Marchlewska, M., Golec de Zavala, A., & Olechowski, M. (2016). 'They will not control us': Ingroup positivity and belief in intergroup conspiracies. *British Journal of Psychology, 107,* 556–576.

Clark, N. (2019, March 29). Brexit Day march: Thousands of pro-Brexit protesters shut down Westminster on what should have been our independence day. *The Sun.* Retrieved from https://www.thesun.co.uk/news/brexit/8750077/thousands-of-pro-brexit-protesters-shut-down-westminster-on-what-should-have-been-our-independence-day/.

Cohen, N. (2018, July 12). How the BBC lost the plot on Brexit. *New York Review of Books.* Retrieved from https://www.nybooks.com/daily/2018/07/12/how-the-bbc-lost-the-plot-on-brexit/.

Collinson, P. (2018, February 26). Overall UK happiness levels given English boost, ONS says. *The Guardian.* Retrieved from https://www.theguardian.com

com/world/2018/feb/26/overall-uk-happiness-level-given-boost-by-english-office-national-statistics-life-satisfaction-survey.

Cooper, R. (2016, August 12). Here's everything Nigel Farage's shit new moustache looks like. *Her.* Retrieved from https://www.her.ie/news/heres-everything-nigel-farages-shit-new-moustache-looks-like-306961.

Coward, R. (2017, March 28). Theresa May takes empty rhetoric to a new level. *The Guardian.* Retrieved from https://www.theguardian.com/commentisfree/2017/mar/28/theresa-may-rhetoric-brexit-authoritarian-delusions.

Crace, J. (2016, November 8). Theresa struggles to take back control—From her own Maybot. *The Guardian.* Retrieved from https://www.theguardian.com/politics/2016/nov/08/theresa-may-struggles-take-back-control-maybot-india-brexit.

Crawford, J. T. (2012). The ideologically objectionable premise model: Predicting biased political judgments on the left and right. *Journal of Experimental Social Psychology, 48,* 138–151.

Crerar, P. (2018, May 29). Labour MPs' fear of Brexit voters could be unfounded, study says. *The Guardian.* Retrieved from https://www.theguardian.com/politics/2018/may/29/labour-mps-fear-brexit-voters-unfounded-study.

Crisp, J. (2016, March 15). *British EPP compares Brexit ballot paper to Hitler's rigged voting slips.* Euractiv. Retrieved from https://www.euractiv.com/section/uk-europe/news/british-epp-compares-brexit-ballot-paper-to-hitlers-rigged-voting-slips/.

Cromby, J. (2019). The myths of Brexit. *Journal of Community & Applied Social Psychology, 29,* 56–66.

Cunningham, J. A., Neighbors, C., Wild, T. C., & Humphreys, K. (2012). Normative misperceptions about alcohol use in a general population sample of problem drinkers from a large metropolitan city. *Alcohol and Alcoholism, 47,* 63–66.

Curtice, J. (2018, August 10). *How young and old would vote on Brexit now.* BBC. Retrieved from https://www.bbc.com/news/uk-politics-45098550.

Curtice, J. (2019, February 11). *Has there been a shift in support for Brexit?* UK in a Changing Europe. Retrieved from https://ukandeu.ac.uk/has-there-been-a-shift-in-support-for-brexit/.

Damasio, H. (2005). Disorders of social conduct following damage to prefrontal cortices. In J. P. Changeux, A. R. Damasio, & W. Singer (Eds.), *Neurobiology of human values* (pp. 37–46). Heidelberg: Springer.

Davidson, T. (2019, March 20). Overheard voice at the end of Theresa May's speech says what we're all thinking. *Mirror.* Retrieved from https://www.mirror.co.uk/news/politics/overheard-voice-end-theresa-mays-14165355.

Davis, C. (2018, December 14). 'Stop calling me INSANE!' *Economist SHUTS down remainer as he calls for no deal Brexit.* Express. Retrieved from https://www.express.co.uk/news/uk/1058613/Brexit-news-latest-deal-vote-Theresa-May-BBC-today-referendum-backstop-debate-row.

Degerman, D. (2018). Brexit anxiety: A case study in the medicalization of dissent. *Critical Review of International Social and Political Philosophy, 8,* 1–18.

Degerman, D. (2019, April 3). *Brexit anxiety shouldn't be over-medicalised: It is fuelling real political engagement.* The Conversation. Retrieved from https://theconversation.com/brexit-anxiety-shouldnt-be-over-medicalised-it-is-fuelling-real-political-engagement-114664.

Del Vicario, M., Zollo, F., Caldarelli, G., Scala, A., & Quattrociocchi, W. (2017). Mapping social dynamics on Facebook: The Brexit debate. *Social Networks, 50,* 6–16.

Dolan, J., Deckman, M. M., & Swers, M. L. (2017). *Women in politics: Paths to power and political influence.* Lanham: Rowman & Littlefield.

Dominiczak, P., & Wilkinson, M. (2016). Theresa May says Britain must look beyond Europe—As she vows to trigger article 50 by March. *Telegraph.* Retrieved from https://www.telegraph.co.uk/news/2016/10/02/theresa-may-brexit-boris-johnson-david-davis-liam-fox-live/.

Dorling, D. (2016). Brexit: The decision of a divided country. *BMJ, 354,* i3697.

Dorling, D., & Tomlinson, S. (2019). *Rule Britannia: Brexit and the end of empire.* London: Biteback.

Downs, A. (1957). *An economic theory of democracy.* New York: Harper.

Duarte, J. L., Crawford, J. T., Stern, C., Haidt, J., Jussim, L., & Tetlock, P. E. (2015). Political diversity will improve social psychological science. *Behavioral and Brain Sciences, 38,* e130.

Duell, M. (2016, August 12). 'On behalf of all people with facial hair, I'd like to complain about Farage's moustache': Twitter melts down at sight of ex-Ukip leader's new 'tache. *Daily Mail.* Retrieved from https://www.dailymail.co.uk/news/article-3736326/Farage-s-moustache-worse-Brexit-Twitter-goes-meltdown-Nigel-Farage-appears-TV-sporting-bushy-new-tache-Ron-Burgundy-proud-of.html.

Dunt, I. (2019, February 1). The collective madness behind Britain's latest Brexit plan. *Washington Post.* Retrieved from https://www.washingtonpost.com/outlook/the-collective-madness-behind-britains-latest-brexit-plan/2019/01/31/48d4d67e-2578-11e9-81fd-b7b05d5bed90_story.html.

Dunyach, J.-F. (2019, January 25). Brexit : «L'empire, thème de choix des eurosceptiques». *Le Monde.* Retrieved from https://www.lemonde.fr/idees/

article/2019/01/25/brexit-l-empire-theme-de-choix-des-eurosceptiques_5414551_3232.html.

Eagly, A. H., Makhijani, M. G., & Klonsky, B. G. (1992). Gender and the evaluation of leaders: A meta-analysis. *Psychological Bulletin, 111*, 3–22.

Earle, S. (2017, October 5). The toxic nostalgia of Brexit. *The Atlantic*. Retrieved from https://www.theatlantic.com/international/archive/2017/10/brexit-britain-may-johnson-eu/542079/.

Eaton, G. (2018, September 12). *Ian Kershaw: 'Brexit would be the greatest act of national self-harm in postwar history'*. *New Statesman*. Retrieved from https://www.newstatesman.com/culture/observations/2018/09/ian-kershaw-brexit-would-be-greatest-act-national-self-harm-postwar.

Edgington, T. (2019, January 15). *What are the biggest government defeats?* BBC. Retrieved from https://www.bbc.com/news/uk-46879887.

Edwardes, C. (2017, October 18). How Jeremy Corbyn transformed into a credible contender for power. *Evening Standard*. Retrieved from https://www.standard.co.uk/lifestyle/esmagazine/how-labour-leader-jeremy-corbyn-transformed-into-a-credible-contender-for-power-a3659826.html.

Ehrenreich, B. (2009). *Smile or die: How positive thinking fooled America and the world*. London: Granta.

Elan, P. (2016, August 15). Gyllenhaal, Franco…Farage? The return of the 70s porntache. *The Guardian*. Retrieved from https://www.theguardian.com/fashion/2016/aug/15/gyllenhaal-franco-farage-the-return-of-the-70s-pornstache.

Electoral Commission. (2015). *Referendum on membership of the European Union: Assessment of the Electoral Commission on the proposed referendum question*. London: Electoral Commission.

El-Enany, N. (2017, May 2). *Things fall apart: From empire to Brexit Britain*. Institute for Policy Research, University of Bath. Retrieved from http://blogs.bath.ac.uk/iprblog/2017/05/02/things-fall-apart-from-empire-to-brexit-britain/.

Elgot, J. (2018, July 17). Vote Leave fined and reported to police by Electoral Commission. *The Guardian*. Retrieved from https://www.theguardian.com/politics/2018/jul/17/vote-leave-fined-and-reported-to-police-by-electoral-commission-brexit.

Elliott, L. (2019, January 30). Pound falls after Commons vote spurs no-deal Brexit fears. *The Guardian*. Retrieved from https://www.theguardian.com/business/2019/jan/30/pound-falls-after-commons-vote-spurs-no-deal-brexit-fears.

Embury-Dennis, T. (2018, September 6). Northern Ireland secretary admits she did not realise nationalists refuse to vote for unionist parties when she took job. *The Independent*. Retrieved from https://www.independent.co.uk/news/

uk/politics/northern-ireland-karen-bradley-secretary-nationalists-unionists-sinn-fein-dup-elections-a8526466.html.

Evans, G., & Schaffner, F. (2019, January 22). *Brexit identities: How Leave versus Remain replaced Conservative versus Labour affiliations of British voters.* The Conversation. Retrieved from https://theconversation.com/brexit-identities-how-leave-versus-remain-replaced-conservative-versus-labour-affiliations-of-british-voters-110311.

Feltham, C. (2016). *Depressive realism: Interdisciplinary perspectives.* London: Routledge.

Ferry, F., Bunting, B., Murphy, S., O'Neill, S., Stein, D., & Koenen, K. (2013). Traumatic events and their relative PTSD burden in Northern Ireland: A consideration of the impact of the 'Troubles'. *Social Psychiatry and Psychiatric Epidemiology, 49,* 435–446.

Flint, C. (2019, February 5). Parliament voted to get a Brexit deal done now. So let's make it happen. *The Guardian.* Retrieved from https://www.theguardian.com/commentisfree/2019/feb/05/parliament-vote-brexit-deal-now.

Flynn, D. J., Nyhan, B., & Reifler, J. (2017). The nature and origins of misperceptions: Understanding false and unsupported beliefs about politics. *Political Psychology, 38,* 127–150.

Ford, R. (2018, October 18). *So in the case of Caroline Flint's Don Valley, 68% *of those who voted* in 2016 backed Brexit (per Chris Hanretty's estimates). But that's actually only 41% of the constituents in her seat. Another 40% didn't vote at all. And that''s *eligible* constituents, not everyone...* [Twitter Post]. Retrieved from https://twitter.com/robfordmancs/status/1052865917628100613.

Foster, P. (2017, March 10). How will Brexit affect Scotland and Northern Ireland? *Telegraph.* Retrieved from https://www.telegraph.co.uk/news/0/how-would-brexit-affect-northern-ireland-and-scotland/.

Fox, F. S. (2016, October 19). Brexit means stupid: So who voted for this? *Mirror.* Retrieved from https://www.mirror.co.uk/news/uk-news/brexit-means-stupid-who-voted-9078503.

Frasquilho, D., Matos, M. G., Salonna, F., Guerreiro, D., Storti, C. C., Gaspar, T., & Caldas-de-Almeida, J. M. (2016). Mental health outcomes in times of economic recession: A systematic literature review. *BMC Public Health, 16,* 115.

Friedman, T. L. (2019, April 2). The United Kingdom has gone mad. *New York Times.* Retrieved from https://www.nytimes.com/2019/04/02/opinion/brexit-news.html.

Gill, A. A. (2016, June 12). Brexit: AA Gill argues for 'In'. *The Times*. Retrieved from https://www.thetimes.co.uk/article/aa-gill-argues-the-case-against-brexit-kmnp83zrt.

Gillett, F. (2017, May 2). Diane Abbott interview: The full transcript of the Shadow Home Secretary's car crash LBC appearance. *Evening Standard*. Retrieved from https://www.standard.co.uk/news/politics/diane-abbott-interview-the-full-transcript-of-the-shadow-home-secretarys-car-crash-lbc-appearance-a3528301.html.

Godlee, F., Kinnair, D., & Nagpaul, C. (2018). Brexit will damage health. *BMJ, 363*, k4804.

Goldberg, D. P., & Williams, P. (1988). *A users' guide to the general health questionnaire*. London: GL Assessment.

Goodwin, M., & Heath, O. (2016, August 31). Brexit vote explained: Poverty, low skills and lack of opportunities. *Joseph Rowntree Foundation*. Retrieved from https://www.jrf.org.uk/report/brexit-vote-explained-poverty-low-skills-and-lack-opportunities.

Green, D. A. (2017, August 3). The tale of the Brexit referendum question. *Financial Times*. Retrieved from https://www.ft.com/content/b56b2b36-1835-37c6-8152-b175cf077ae8.

Green, G., & Gilbertson, J. (2008). *Warm front better health: Health impact evaluation of the Warm Front scheme*. Sheffield: Centre for Regional, Economic and Social Research, Sheffield Hallam University.

Greenglass, E. R., Katter, J. K., Fiksenbaum, L., & Hughes, B. M. (2015). Surviving in difficult economic times: Relationship between economic factors, self-esteem and psychological distress in university students. In R. J. Burke, C. L. Cooper, & A.-S. G. Antoniou (Eds.), *The multi-generational and aging workforce: Challenges and opportunities* (pp. 58–77). Cheltenham: Edward Elgar.

Hanretty, C. (2017). Areal interpolation and the UK's referendum on EU membership. *Journal of Elections, Public Opinion and Parties, 27*, 466–483.

Hänska-Ahy, M., & Bauchowitz, S. (2017). Tweeting for Brexit: How social media influenced the referendum. In J. Mair, T. Clark, N. Fowler, R. Snoddy, & R. Tait (Eds.), *Brexit, Trump and the media* (pp. 31–35). Bury St Edmunds: Abramis.

Harding, R. (2017). *British social attitudes* (Vol. 34). London: NatCen.

Harris, T. (2019, January 22). Remainers won't 'get' Brexit until they understand their caricature of Brexiteers is entirely wrong. *BrexitCentral*. Retrieved from https://brexitcentral.com/remainers-wont-get-brexit-understand-caricature-brexiteers-entirely-wrong/.

Hart, W., Albarracín, D., Eagly, A. H., Brechan, I., Lindberg, M. J., & Merrill, L. (2009). Feeling validated versus being correct: A meta-analysis of selective exposure to information. *Psychological Bulletin, 135,* 555–588.

Hawker, L. (2019, May 24). *Brexit Party milkshake pensioner fundraising hits £5k as anger grows at conspiracy claims.* Express. Retrieved from https://www. express.co.uk/news/politics/1131638/Brexit-party-milkshake-European-elections-Don-MacNaughton.

Heald, A., Vida, B., Farman, S., & Bhugra, D. (2018). The LEAVE vote and racial abuse towards Black and Minority Ethnic communities across the UK: The impact on mental health. *Journal of the Royal Society of Medicine, 111,* 158–161.

Herrman, J. (2016, June 24). 'Brexit' talk on social media favoured the 'Leave' side. *New York Times.* Retrieved from https://www.nytimes.com/2016/06/25/business/brexit-talk-on-social-media-heavily-favored-the-leave-side.html.

Hilbig, B. E., & Moshagen, M. (2015). A predominance of self-identified Democrats is no evidence of a leftward bias. *Behavioral and Brain Sciences, 38,* e146.

Hills, J. (2019, January 25). Chancellor Philip Hammond says no-deal Brexit would be 'both political betrayal and economic self-harm'. *ITV.* Retrieved from https://www.itv.com/news/2019-01-25/chancellor-philip-hammond-brexit/.

Hills, T. (2019, January 29). 6 negotiation lessons from the Brexit disaster. *Psychology Today.* Retrieved from https://www.psychologytoday.com/intl/blog/statistical-life/201901/6-negotiation-lessons-the-brexit-disaster.

Holbrook, A. L., Krosnick, J. A., Carson, R. T., & Mitchell, R. C. (2000). Violating conversational conventions disrupts cognitive processing of attitude questions. *Journal of Experimental Social Psychology, 36,* 465–494.

Hope, C. (2019, March 16). Commemorative Brexit coins delayed amid confusion over date of departure. *Telegraph.* Retrieved from https://www.telegraph.co.uk/politics/2019/03/16/commemorative-brexit-coins-delayed-amid-confusion-date-departure/.

Hornsey, M. J., & Jetten, J. (2004). The individual within the group: Balancing the need to belong with the need to be different. *Personality and Social Psychology Review, 8,* 248–264.

Horton, H. (2016, August 12). Nigel Farage wows social media with new moustache. *Telegraph.* Retrieved from https://www.telegraph.co.uk/news/2016/08/12/nigel-farage-wows-social-media-with-new-moustache/.

House, R. J., Hanges, P. J., Javidan, M., Dorfman, P. W., & Gupta, V. (Eds.). (2004). *Culture, leadership, and organizations: The GLOBE study of 62 societies.* Thousand Oaks, CA: Sage.

Hughes, B. M. (2004). Life, death, and psychology. *Irish Psychologist, 31,* 158–163.

Hughes, B. M. (2016). *Rethinking psychology: Good science, bad science, pseudoscience.* London: Palgrave.

Hughes, B. M. (2018). *Psychology in crisis.* London: Palgrave.

Hughes, P. (2017, May 12). *Every Leave constituency where the MP voted Remain.* iNews. Retrieved from https://inews.co.uk/news/politics/every-leave-constituency-with-a-remain-mp/.

Hyde, J. S. (2014). Gender similarities and differences. *Annual Review of Psychology, 65,* 373–398.

Inbar, Y., & Lammers, J. (2012). Political diversity in social and personality psychology. *Perspectives on Psychological Science, 7,* 496–503.

Ipsos MORI. (2013). Perceptions are not reality: The top 10 we get wrong. *Ipsos MORI.* Retrieved from https://www.ipsos.com/sites/default/files/migrations/en-uk/files/Assets/Docs/Polls/ipsos-mori-rss-kings-perils-of-perception-methodology-note.pdf.

Ipsos MORI. (2017). *Shifting ground: 8 key findings from a longitudinal study on attitudes towards immigration and Brexit.* London: Ipsos MORI.

Irish Times. (2016, June 24). Irish Times view: Brexit a bewildering act of self-harm. *Irish Times.* Retrieved from https://www.irishtimes.com/opinion/editorial/irish-times-view-brexit-a-bewildering-act-of-self-harm-1.2698212.

Isaac, A. (2019, June 10). Can the economy recover from its 'Brexit hangover'? *Telegraph.* Retrieved from https://www.telegraph.co.uk/business/2019/06/10/can-economy-recover-brexit-hangover/.

Jackson, G. (2018, December 9). How is Brexit uncertainty affecting the UK economy? *Financial Times.* Retrieved from https://www.ft.com/content/1c161ef2-fba9-11e8-ac00-57a2a826423e.

Jackson, L. B. (2017). *Islamophobia in Britain: The making of a Muslim enemy.* Cham, Switzerland: Palgrave Macmillan.

James, E. L. (2012). *Fifty shades of grey.* London: Vintage.

Jamieson, S. (2018, March 11). Brexit vote was 'driven by nostalgia' for a world where 'faces were white', Sir Vince Cable claims. *Telegraph.* Retrieved from https://www.telegraph.co.uk/politics/2018/03/11/brexit-vote-driven-nostalgia-world-faces-white-sir-vince-cable/.

Jenkins, S. (2018, August 30). Hooligan Brexiters now offer a mad, dystopian future nobody voted for. *The Guardian.* Retrieved from https://www.

theguardian.com/commentisfree/2018/aug/30/brexiters-future-crashing-out-hard-soft-brexit-dominic-raab.

Johnson, B. (2018, July 9). *Boris Johnson's resignation letter and May's reply in full.* BBC. Retrieved from https://www.bbc.com/news/uk-politics-44772804.

Johnson, J. H., & Gluck, M. (2016). *Everydata: The misinformation hidden in the little data you consume every day.* New York: Bibliomotion.

Jolley, D., & Douglas, K. M. (2014). The effects of anti-vaccine conspiracy theories on vaccination intentions. *PloS One, 9,* e89177.

Judah, B. (2016, July 12). England's last gasp of empire. *New York Times.* Retrieved from https://www.nytimes.com/2016/07/13/opinion/englands-last-gasp-of-empire.html.

Judd, C. M., & Park, B. (1988). Out-group homogeneity: Judgments of variability at the individual and group levels. *Journal of Personality and Social Psychology, 54,* 778–788.

Judge, T. A., Bono, J. E., Ilies, R., & Gerhardt, M. W. (2002). Personality and leadership: A qualitative and quantitative review. *Journal of Applied Psychology, 87,* 765–780.

Kahan, D. M., Jenkins-Smith, H., & Braman, D. (2011). Cultural cognition of scientific consensus. *Journal of Risk Research, 14,* 147–174.

Kaniasty, K., & Norris, F. H. (2004). Social support in the aftermath of disasters, catastrophes, and acts of terrorism: Altruistic, overwhelmed, uncertain, antagonistic, and patriotic communities. In R. Ursano, A. Norwood, & C. Fullerton (Eds.), *Bioterrorism: Psychological and public health interventions* (pp. 200–229). Cambridge: Cambridge University Press.

Kaniasty, K., & Norris, F. H. (2009). Distinctions that matter: Received social support, perceived social support, and social embeddedness after disasters. In Y. Neria, S. Galea, & F. Norris (Eds.), *Mental health and disasters* (pp. 175–202). Cambridge: Cambridge University Press.

Kelly, J. (2016, June 29). *Branger. Debression. Oexit. Zumxit. Why did Brexit trigger a brexplosion of wordplay?* Slate. Retrieved from https://slate.com/human-interest/2016/06/why-has-brexit-sparked-an-explosion-of-wordplay.html.

Kennedy, D. (2018, December 17). *Brexit and the legacies of empire* [Audio]. Soundcloud. Retrieved from https://soundcloud.com/history-policy/dane-kennedy.

Kenny, K. (2005). *Ireland and the British Empire.* Oxford: Oxford University Press.

Kentish, B. (2017, September 17). Boris Johnson 'misused' figures with £350m Brexit claim, UK statistics chief says. *The Independent.* Retrieved from https://www.independent.co.uk/news/uk/politics/boris-johnson-350m-brexit-nhs-misled-uk-statistics-authority-the-telegraph-sir-david-norgrove-amber-a7951711.html.

Kentish, B. (2018, September 17). Leave voters dying and remainers reaching voting age means majority will soon oppose Brexit, study finds. *The Independent*. Retrieved from https://www.independent.co.uk/news/uk/politics/brexit-leave-eu-remain-vote-support-against-poll-uk-europe-final-say-yougov-second-referendum-peter-a8541971.html.

Khaleeli, H. (2016, June 29). 'A frenzy of hatred': How to understand Brexit racism. *The Guardian*. Retrieved from https://www.theguardian.com/politics/2016/jun/29/frenzy-hatred-brexit-racism-abuse-referendum-celebratory-lasting-damage.

Kim, H. (2016). The role of emotions and culture in the third-person effect process of news coverage of election poll results. *Communication Research, 43,* 109–130.

Kruger, J., & Dunning, D. (1999). Unskilled and unaware of it: How difficulties in recognizing one's own incompetence lead to inflated self-assessments. *Journal of Personality and Social Psychology, 77,* 1121–1134.

Kruglanski, A. W., & Webster, D. M. (1996). Motivated closing of the mind: 'Seizing' and 'freezing'. *Psychological Review, 103,* 263–283.

Kunst, J. R., Thomsen, L., Sam, D. L., & Berry, J. W. (2015). 'We are in this together': Common group identity predicts majority members' active acculturation efforts to integrate immigrants. *Personality and Social Psychology Bulletin, 41,* 1438–1453.

LaFortune, K. A. (2018). Eliminating offensive legal language. *Monitor on Psychology, 49,* 29.

Lally, M. (2019, March 24). Are you suffering from 'Strexit'? *Telegraph*. Retrieved from https://www.telegraph.co.uk/health-fitness/body/suffering-strexit/.

Langer, E. J. (1975). The illusion of control. *Journal of Personality and Social Psychology, 32,* 311–328.

Lawson, D. (2018, September 23). Yes, there can be a second Brexit referendum: In a decade or two. *The Times*. Retrieved from https://www.thetimes.co.uk/article/yes-there-can-be-a-second-brexit-referendum-in-a-decade-or-two-srcnqpw3c.

Laycock, S. (2012). *All the countries we've ever invaded: And the few we never got round to*. Stroud: History Press.

Lee, G. (2018, November 26). *FactCheck: May isn't telling the whole story on immigration*. Channel 4. Retrieved from https://www.channel4.com/news/factcheck/factcheck-may-isnt-telling-the-whole-story-on-immigration.

Letts, Q. (2017). *Patronising bastards: How the elites betrayed Britain.* London: Constable.

Levy, D. A. L., Aslan, B., & Bironzo, D. (2016). *UK press coverage of the EU referendum.* Oxford: Reuters Institute.

Lichfield, J. (2017, September 18). Boris Johnson's £350m claim is devious and bogus: Here's why. *The Guardian.* Retrieved from https://www.theguardian.com/commentisfree/2017/sep/18/boris-johnson-350-million-claim-bogus-foreign-secretary.

Lis, J. (2019, May 16). Brexit and the schoolboy fantasy that we can rule the world without really trying. *Prospect Magazine.* Retrieved from https://www.prospectmagazine.co.uk/politics/brexit-schoolboy-fantasy-rule-the-world-european-elections-european-union.

Liu, C. (2019, April 2). Solving the Brexit deadlock by lottery. *Psychology Today.* Retrieved from https://www.psychologytoday.com/intl/blog/decisions-defined/201904/solving-the-brexit-deadlock-lottery.

Lorenz, J., Rauhut, H., Schweitzer, F., & Helbing, D. (2011). How social influence can undermine the wisdom of crowd effect. *PNAS, 108,* 9020–9025.

Lusher, A. (2017, August 13). Saviour of the Tory party or 'reactionary poison'? Will Jacob Rees-Mogg run for Tory leader, and what would he do as PM? *The Independent.* Retrieved from https://www.independent.co.uk/news/uk/politics/jacob-rees-mogg-moggmentum-run-for-tory-leader-leadership-election-contest-conservative-party-a7891196.html.

Lyons, K. (2016, June 26). Racist incidents feared to be linked to Brexit result. *The Guardian.* Retrieved from https://www.theguardian.com/politics/2016/jun/26/racist-incidents-feared-to-be-linked-to-brexit-result-reported-in-england-and-wales.

Mac Cormaic, R. (2018, December 15). Remainers should not be let off the hook on Brexit. *Irish Times.* Retrieved from https://www.irishtimes.com/opinion/remainers-should-not-be-let-off-the-hook-on-brexit-1.3731493.

Mackey, R. P. (2016, June 21). *Gove: Britons 'have had enough of experts'* [Video]. Retrieved from YouTube: http://y2u.be/GGgiGtJk7MA.

Mance, H. (2016, June 3). Britain has had enough of experts, says Gove. *Financial Times.* Retrieved from https://www.ft.com/content/3be49734-29cb-11e6-83e4-abc22d5d108c.

Mance, H. (2017, August 1). Most Brexiters say economic damage is a 'price worth paying'. *Financial Times.* Retrieved from https://www.ft.com/content/1b636ba8-76b3-11e7-a3e8-60495fe6ca71.

Manley, J. (2018, June 28). Lord Patten says Brexit will damage Britain and Ireland. *Irish News.* Retrieved from http://www.irishnews.com/news/northernirelandnews/2018/06/28/lord-patten-says-brexit-will-damage-britain-and-ireland-1368070.

Marchlewska, M., Cichocka, A., & Kossowska, M. (2018). Addicted to answers: Need for cognitive closure and the endorsement of conspiracy beliefs. *European Journal of Social Psychology, 48,* 109–117.

Marsh, E. J., & Yang, B. W. (2018). Believing things that are not true: A cognitive science perspective on misinformation. In B. G. Southwell, E. A. Thorson, & L. Shelbe (Eds.), *Misinformation and mass audiences* (pp. 15–34). Austin: University of Texas Press.

Martínez-Miranda, J., & Aldea, A. (2005). Emotions in human and artificial intelligence. *Computers in Human Behavior, 21,* 323–341.

Mason, P. (2018, March 13). Delusions, hypocrisy and historical amnesia: The Tory Brexit meltdown begins here. *New Statesman.* Retrieved from https://www.newstatesman.com/politics/brexit/2018/03/delusions-hypocrisy-and-historical-amnesia-tory-brexit-meltdown-begins-here.

Matsumoto, D., & Willingham, B. (2006). The thrill of victory and the agony of defeat: Spontaneous expressions of medal winners of the 2004 Athens Olympic Games. *Journal of Personality and Social Psychology, 91,* 568–581.

McAlpine, D. D., McCreedy, E., & Alang, S. (2018). The meaning and predictive value of self-rated mental health among persons with a mental health problem. *Journal of Health and Social Behavior, 59,* 200–214.

McGarty, C., Turner, J. C., Hogg, M. A., David, B., & Wetherell, M. S. (1992). Group polarization as conformity to the prototypical group member. *British Journal of Social Psychology, 31,* 1–19.

McNulty, J. K., & Fincham, F. D. (2012). Beyond positive psychology? Toward a contextual view of psychological processes and well-being. *American Psychologist, 67,* 101–110.

Mental Health Foundation. (2019, March 21). *Millions have felt 'powerless', 'angry' or 'worried' because of Brexit: Results of our new poll.* Mental Health. Retrieved from https://www.mentalhealth.org.uk/news/millions-have-felt-powerless-angry-or-worried-because-brexit-results-our-new-poll.

Meredith, J., & Richardson, E. (2019). The use of the political categories of Brexiter and Remainer in online comments about the EU referendum. *Journal of Community and Applied Social Psychology, 29,* 43–55.

Merrick, R. (2018, November 8). Brexit secretary Dominic Raab says he 'hadn't quite understood' importance of Dover-Calais crossing. *The Independent.* Retrieved from https://www.independent.co.uk/news/uk/politics/brexit-latest-dominic-raab-trade-eu-france-calais-dover-economy-finance-deal-a8624036.html.

Merrick, R. (2019, February 7). Brexit: Young people 'will neither forget nor forgive' Leave campaigners, warns John Major. *The Independent.* Retrieved from https://www.independent.co.uk/news/uk/politics/brexit-young-people-voters-second-referendum-final-say-john-major-eu-remain-a8767666.html.

Miranda, C. (2016, June 25). The empire strikes back: Cameron quits over Brexit loss. *The Daily Telegraph.* Sydney. Retrieved from: https://www.pressreader.com/australia/the-daily-telegraph-sydney/20160625/textview.

Mitchell, B., & Roberts, J. V. (2012). Sentencing for murder: Exploring public knowledge and public opinion in England and Wales. *British Journal of Criminology, 52,* 141–158.

Moody, A. (2013). Adult anthropometric measures, overweight and obesity. In R. Craig & J. Mindell (Eds.), *Health survey for England: 2012.* London: Health and Social Care Information Centre.

Murtagh, P. (2019, January 21). 'Do I need two vets now?' Border farmers sweat over Brexit. *Irish Times.* Retrieved from https://www.irishtimes.com/news/ireland/irish-news/do-i-need-two-vets-now-border-farmers-sweat-over-brexit-1.3764466.

Myerson, R. B. (1991). *Game theory: Analysis of conflict.* Boston: Harvard University Press.

Nair, A. (2017, March 17). *'Boring' Bob Geldof brands Brexit 'greatest act of self-harm' and vows to 'undermine'* May. Express. Retrieved from https://www.express.co.uk/news/uk/780132/Bob-Geldof-shuns-Brexit-self-harm-vows-to-undermine-Theresa-May-bbc-nolan-live.

Ní Aodha, G. (2018, December 31). The ridiculous things UK politicians have said about Ireland and Brexit. *The Journal.* Retrieved from https://www.thejournal.ie/uk-politicians-4336217-Dec2018/.

Norton, M. I., Mochon, D., & Ariely, D. (2012). The IKEA effect: When labor leads to love. *Journal of Consumer Psychology, 22,* 453–460.

Nyhan, B., & Reifler, J. (2010). When corrections fail: Persistence of political misperceptions. *Political Behavior, 32,* 303–330.

O'Connor, R. C., Wetherall, K., Cleare, S., Eschle, S., Drummond, J., Ferguson, E., … O'Carroll, R. E. (2018). Suicide attempts and non-suicidal self-harm: National prevalence study of young adults. *BJPsych Open, 4,* 142–148.

O'Donoghue, D. (2019, May 17). Theresa May's Brexit strategy akin to 'masochism'. *Press and Journal.* Retrieved from https://www.pressandjournal.co.uk/fp/news/politics/westminster/1750363/theresa-mays-brexit-strategy-akin-to-masochism/.

O'Neill, S. (2019). Brexit and Northern Ireland: Leaders must consider the mental health of the population. *Lancet: Psychiatry, 6*, 372–373.

O'Toole, F. (2018). *Heroic failure: Brexit and the politics of pain*. London: Head of Zeus.

Oikonomou, G. (2017, August 24). *My views on the #UKgov papers: #Brexit does not mean Brexit shar.es/1SGmyq @icmacentre @HenleyBSchool* [Twitter Post]. Retrieved from: https://twitter.com/i_oikonomou/status/900751417346064384.

Olusoga, D. (2017, March 19). Empire 2.0 is dangerous nostalgia for something that never existed. *The Guardian*. Retrieved from https://www.theguardian.com/commentisfree/2017/mar/19/empire-20-is-dangerous-nostalgia-for-something-that-never-existed.

Oppenheim, M. (2017, July 11). James O'Brien demolishes Leave voter in farcical on-air standoff. *The Independent*. Retrieved from https://www.independent.co.uk/news/uk/home-news/james-o-brien-leave-voter-lbc-radio-on-air-live-brexit-brexiteer-argument-call-in-standoff-a7835011.html.

Orbach, S. (2016, July 1). Susie Orbach: In therapy, everyone wants to talk about Brexit. *The Guardian*. Retrieved from https://www.theguardian.com/global/2016/jul/01/susie-orbach-in-therapy-everyone-wants-to-talk-about-brexit.

Owen, G. (2019, June 2). *Truss: Only Johnson has the 'oomph' to be leader*. MailOnline. Retrieved from https://www.dailymail.co.uk/news/article-7094851/Boris-Johnson-backed-Liz-Truss-week-ruled-race-Tory-leader.html.

Park, J., & Hill, W. T. (2018). Exploring the role of justification and cognitive effort exertion on post-purchase regret in online shopping. *Computers in Human Behavior, 83*, 235–242.

Payne, A. (2016, August 12). *Nigel Farage has grown a moustache and the internet can't handle it*. Business Insider. Retrieved from https://www.businessinsider.com/nigel-farage-moustache-ukip-2016-8.

Pearson, A. (2018, November 20). It's beginning to look a lot like a Brexit conspiracy. *Telegraph*. Retrieved from https://www.telegraph.co.uk/politics/2018/11/20/beginning-look-lot-like-brexit-conspiracy/.

Peck, T. (2019, March 20). With the single worst speech she has ever given, Theresa May shifted all the blame for the failure of Brexit on to herself. *The Independent*. Retrieved from https://www.independent.co.uk/voices/theresa-may-brexit-speech-failure-withdrawal-agreement-donald-tusk-meaningful-vote-downing-street-a8832741.html.

Peel, Q. (2016, September 19). Historic misunderstanding underlies UK-EU relationship on Churchill anniversary. *Financial Times*. Retrieved from https://www.ft.com/content/3d6bbabc-7122-11e6-a0c9-1365ce54b926.

Pettifor, A. (2016). Brexit and its consequences. *Globalizations, 14,* 127–132.

Polage, D. C. (2012). Making up history: False memories of fake news stories. *Europe's Journal of Psychology, 8,* 245–250.

Powdthavee, N., Plagnol, A. C., Frijters, P., & Clark, A. E. (2019). Who got the Brexit blues? The effect of Brexit on subjective wellbeing in the UK. *Economica, 86,* 471–494.

Prynn, J. (2016, July 11). 'Brexit anxiety' brings queue of patients for psychiatrists. *Evening Standard.* Retrieved from https://www.standard.co.uk/news/politics/brexit-anxiety-brings-queue-of-patients-for-psychiatrists-a3292746.html.

Pryor, C., Perfors, A., & Howe, P. D. L. (2018). Reversing the endowment effect. *Judgment and Decision Making, 13,* 275–286.

Purnell, S. (2014, August 6). Boris Johnson's carefully cultivated clownish image masks a self-centred and ruthlessly ambitious man. *Mirror.* Retrieved from https://www.mirror.co.uk/news/uk-news/boris-johnsons-carefully-cultivated-clownish-4005821.

Quinn, B. (2019, June 25). Gordon Brown: Unity of UK at risk from 'hijacking of patriotism'. *The Guardian.* Retrieved from https://www.theguardian.com/politics/2019/jun/25/gordon-brown-unity-of-uk-at-risk-from-hijacking-of-patriotism-brexit.

Rae, A. (2016, June 25). *What can explain Brexit?* Stats, Maps n Pix. Retrieved from http://www.statsmapsnpix.com/2016/06/what-can-explain-brexit.html.

Randerson, J. (2019, January 24). *Leo Varadkar: Brexit was 'not fully thought through'.* Politico. Retrieved from https://www.politico.eu/article/leo-varakar-brexit-was-not-fully-thought-through/.

Rawnsley, A. (2019a, May 26). What makes the Tories think that anyone must be better than Mrs May? *The Guardian.* Retrieved from https://www.theguardian.com/commentisfree/2019/may/26/what-makes-tories-think-anyone-must-be-better-than-theresa-may.

Rawnsley, A. (2019b, May 19). The middle ground no longer exists over Brexit: It's all or nothing now. *The Guardian.* Retrieved from https://www.theguardian.com/commentisfree/2019/may/19/the-middle-ground-no-longer-exists-over-brexit-its-all-or-nothing-now.

Read, C. (2019, April 12). *BREXHAUSTION: Health warning issued due to Brexit stress.* Express. Retrieved from https://www.express.co.uk/news/politics/1113602/brexit-news-health-stress.

Redding, R. E. (2001). Sociopolitical diversity in psychology: The case for pluralism. *American Psychologist, 56,* 205–215.

Reicher, S. (2004). The context of social identity: Domination, resistance, and change. *Political Psychology, 25*, 921–945.

Richards, B. (2019). *The psychology of politics.* London: Routledge.

Richards, L., & Heath, A. (2019, January 31). *Brexit and public opinion: National identity and Brexit preferences.* UK in a Changing Europe. Retrieved from https://ukandeu.ac.uk/brexit-and-public-opinion-national-identity-and-brexit-preferences/.

Ridley, L. (2016, July 2). *Racism after Brexit is 'celebratory' and 'Englishness' is becoming exclusively white and Christian, says expert.* HuffPost. Retrieved from https://www.huffingtonpost.co.uk/entry/racism-after-brexit-attacks-muslims-leave_uk_57766dc8e4b0f7b55795302d.

Rogers, I. (2019). *9 lessons in Brexit.* London: Short Books.

Rogers, J. F., & Ostfeld, R. (2017, December 6). *Environmentalism and the value-action gap.* YouGov. Retrieved from https://yougov.co.uk/topics/science/articles-reports/2017/12/06/environmentalism-value-action-gap.

Russo, L. (2017). The use of aggregate data in the study of voting behavior: Ecological inference, ecological fallacy and other applications. In J. Fisher, E. Fieldhouse, M. N. Franklin, R. Gibson, M. Cantijoch, & C. Wlezien (Eds.), *The Routledge handbook of elections, voting behavior and public opinion.* London: Routledge.

Ryan, M. K., & Haslam, S. A. (2007). The glass cliff: Exploring the dynamics surrounding the appointment of women to precarious leadership positions. *Academy of Management Review, 32*, 549–572.

Sabbagh, D., & Elgot, J. (2018, December 10). Theresa May postpones Brexit deal vote. *The Guardian.* Retrieved from https://www.theguardian.com/politics/2018/dec/10/theresa-may-postpones-brexit-deal-meaningful-vote-eu.

Samuelson, R. J. (2016, May 1). Britain flirts with economic insanity. *Washington Post.* Retrieved from https://www.washingtonpost.com/opinions/britain-flirts-with-economic-insanity/2016/05/01/bb8d7a4a-0e1f-11e6-bfa1-4efa856caf2a_story.html.

Sandhu, S. (2018, July 8). *Every Remain-voting constituency with a pro-Brexit MP.* iNews. Retrieved from https://inews.co.uk/news/politics/pro-brexit-mps-represent-remain-constituencies/.

Saunders, R. (2019, January 7). The myth of Brexit as imperial nostalgia. *Prospect Magazine.* Retrieved from https://www.prospectmagazine.co.uk/world/the-myth-of-brexit-as-imperial-nostalgia.

Savage, M. (2017, May 7). Theresa May pledges mental health revolution will reduce detentions. *The Guardian.* Retrieved from https://www.theguardian.

com/politics/2017/may/07/theresa-may-pledges-mental-health-revolution-will-reduce-detentions.

Schachter, S., & Singer, J. (1962). Cognitive, social, and physiological determinants of emotional state. *Psychological Review, 69,* 379–399.

Scott, P. (2019, January 16). Theresa May's withdrawal bill just became biggest ever government defeat in the House of Commons. *Telegraph.* Retrieved from https://www.telegraph.co.uk/politics/2019/01/16/theresa-mays-withdrawal-bill-just-became-biggest-ever-government/.

Sheehan, M. (2018, December 17). Irish army identifies 300 border crossing points. *Belfast Telegraph.* Retrieved from https://www.belfasttelegraph.co.uk/news/northern-ireland/irish-army-identifies-300-border-crossing-points-37631474.html.

Shipman, T. (2016). *All out war: The full story of Brexit.* London: William Collins.

Shipman, T. (2017). *Fall out: A year of political mayhem.* London: William Collins.

Shrimsley, R. (2018, July 19). Brexit, Boris and the perils of positive thinking. *Financial Times.* Retrieved from https://www.ft.com/content/3419e61c-8a18-11e8-bf9e-8771d5404543.

Sibley, C. G., Osborne, D., & Duckitt, J. (2012). Personality and political orientation: Meta-analysis and test of a threat-constraint model. *Journal of Research in Personality, 46,* 664–677.

Smith, M. (2017a, March 10). *Beards are growing on the British public.* YouGov. Retrieved from https://yougov.co.uk/topics/politics/articles-reports/2017/03/10/beards-are-growing-british-public.

Smith, M. (2017b, March 13). *Would you Adam and Eve it? A fifth of Londoners failed YouGov's cockney rhyming slang test.* YouGov. Retrieved from https://yougov.co.uk/topics/politics/articles-reports/2017/06/06/how-british-fictional-characters-might-vote-2017-g.

Smith, M. (2017c, June 6). *How British fictional characters might vote: 2017 general election edition.* YouGov. Retrieved from: https://yougov.co.uk/topics/politics/articles-reports/2017/06/06/how-british-fictional-characters-might-vote-2017-g.

Smith, M. (2019, May 6). The unspoken truth: Brexit is so bad it is funny. *Village Magazine.* Retrieved from https://villagemagazine.ie/index.php/2019/05/the-unspoken-truth-brexit-is-so-bad-it-is-funny/.

Son Hing, L. S., Bobocel, D. R., Zanna, M. P., & McBride, M. V. (2007). Authoritarian dynamics and unethical decision making: High social dominance orientation leaders and high right-wing authoritarianism followers. *Journal of Personality and Social Psychology, 92,* 67–81.

Spicer, A. (2016, July 1). The UK is in Brexistential crisis. Is there a way forward? *The Guardian*. Retrieved from https://www.theguardian.com/commentisfree/2016/jul/01/uk-brexit-brexistential-vote-leave-eu-britain.

Stern, C., West, T. V., Jost, J. T., & Rule, N. O. (2014). 'Ditto heads': Do conservatives perceive greater consensus within their ranks than liberals? *Personality and Social Psychology Bulletin, 40*, 1162–1177.

Stevens, J. (2016, June 28). NHS trust offers nurses and mental health carers free counselling to get over the referendum vote. *Daily Mail*. Retrieved from https://www.dailymail.co.uk/news/article-3664762/NHS-trust-offers-nurses-mental-health-carers-free-counselling-referendum-vote.html#comments.

Stewart, H. (2019, January 16). May suffers heaviest parliamentary defeat of a British PM in the democratic era. *The Guardian*. Retrieved from https://www.theguardian.com/politics/2019/jan/15/theresa-may-loses-brexit-deal-vote-by-majority-of-230.

Stewart, H., & Mason, R. (2016, April 7). EU referendum: £9m taxpayer-funded publicity blitz pushes case to remain. *The Guardian*. Retrieved from https://www.theguardian.com/politics/2016/apr/06/cameron-to-push-case-remain-eu-with-9m-taxpayer-funded-publicity-blitz.

Stewart, H., Mason, R., & Walker, P. (2019, March 28). Brexit: May vows to resign before next phase of negotiations if deal is passed. *The Guardian*. Retrieved from https://www.theguardian.com/politics/2019/mar/27/theresa-may-to-resign-before-next-phase-of-brexit.

Stiensmeier-Pelster, J., & Heckhausen, H. (2018). Causal attribution of behavior and achievement. In J. Heckhausen & H. Heckhausen (Eds.), *Motivation and action*. New York: Springer.

Strack, F., & Mussweiler, T. (1997). Explaining the enigmatic anchoring effect: Mechanisms of selective accessibility. *Journal of Personality and Social Psychology, 73*, 437–446.

Stuckler, D., Basu, S., Suhrcke, M., Coutts, A., & McKee, M. (2011). Effects of the 2008 recession on health: A first look at European data. *Lancet, 378*, 124–125.

Sturridge, P. (2018a). Brexit, British politics, and the left-right divide. *Political Insight, 9*(4), 4–7.

Sturridge, P. (2018b, August 15). *The social roots of values and their influence on voting*. Medium. Retrieved from https://medium.com/@psurridge/the-social-roots-of-values-and-their-influence-on-voting-aae8c193821.

Sumner, C., Scofield, J. E., Buchanan, E. M., Evans, M.-R., & Shearing, M. (2018, July 5). *The role of personality, authoritarianism and cognition in the United Kingdom's 2016 referendum on European Union membership.* Online Privacy Foundation. Retrieved from https://www.onlineprivacyfoundation.org/opf-research/psychological-biases/personality-authoritarianism-and-cognition-in-brexit/.

Tabernero, C., Chambel, M. J., Curral, L., & Arana, J. M. (2009). The role of task-oriented versus relationship-oriented leadership on normative contract and group performance. *Social Behavior and Personality, 37,* 1391–1404.

Taylor, S. E., & Brown, J. D. (1988). Illusion and well-being: A social psychological perspective on mental health. *Psychological Bulletin, 103,* 193–210.

Tharoor, I. (2019, January 4). Fool Britannia: Britain clings to imperial nostalgia as Brexit looms. *Washington Post.* Retrieved from https://www.washingtonpost.com/world/2019/01/04/britain-clings-imperial-nostalgia-brexit-looms/.

Thomas, S. (2016, October 10). Why Brexit is just like having a baby. *Spectator.* Retrieved from https://blogs.spectator.co.uk/2016/10/brexit-just-like-baby/.

Tillman, E. R. (2013). Authoritarianism and citizen attitudes towards European integration. *European Union Politics, 14,* 566–589.

TLDR News. (2019, February 19). *Game theory explains why no deal is inevitable: Brexit explained* [Video]. YouTube. Retrieved from http://y2u.be/BHiT9VPkgUY.

Tombs, R. (2019, May 21). Extreme remainers are driven by a misguided pessimism about Britain's future. *Telegraph.* Retrieved from https://www.telegraph.co.uk/politics/2019/05/21/extreme-remainers-driven-misguided-pessimism-britains-future/.

Turner, J. C., Wetherell, M. S., & Hogg, M. A. (1989). Referent informational influence and group polarization. *British Journal of Social Psychology, 28,* 135–147.

Tversky, A., & Kahneman, D. (1973). Availability: A heuristic for judging frequency and probability. *Cognitive Psychology, 5,* 207–232.

Tversky, A., & Kahneman, D. (1982). Judgments of and by representativeness. In D. Kahneman, P. Slovic, & A. Tversky (Eds.), *Judgment under uncertainty: Heuristics and biases.* Cambridge: Cambridge University Press.

Tversky, A., & Kahneman, D. (1992). Advances in prospect theory: Cumulative representation of uncertainty. *Journal of Risk and Uncertainty, 5,* 297–323.

Van de Vyver, J., Leite, A. C., Abrams, D., & Palmer, S. B. (2018). Brexit or Bremain? A person and social analysis of voting decisions in the EU referendum. *Journal of Community & Applied Social Psychology, 28,* 65–69.

Van der Linden, S., Leiserowitz, A., Rosenthal, S., & Maibach, E. (2017). Inoculating the public against misinformation about climate change. *Global Challenges, 1,* 1600008.

Van Swol, L. M. (2009). Extreme members and group polarization. *Social Influence, 4,* 185–199.

Vandoros, S., Avendano, M., & Kawachi, I. (2019). The EU referendum and mental health in the short term: A natural experiment using antidepressant prescriptions in England. *Journal of Epidemiology & Community Health, 73,* 168–175.

Verweij, M., Senior, T. J., Domínguez, J. F., & Turner, R. (2015). Emotion, rationality, and decision-making: How to link affective and social neuroscience with social theory. *Frontiers in Neuroscience, 9,* 332.

Wagner-Egger, P., Delouvée, S., Gauvrit, N., & Dieguez, S. (2018). Creationism and conspiracism share a common teleological bias. *Current Biology, 28,* R867–R868.

Walker, A. (2019, February 4). Do mention the war: The politicians comparing Brexit to WWII. *The Guardian.* Retrieved from https://www.theguardian.com/politics/2019/feb/04/do-mention-the-war-the-politicians-comparing-brexit-to-wwii.

Walker, P. (2019, June 25). Brexit: Johnson says Britain will leave EU on 31 October 'do or die'. *The Guardian.* Retrieved from https://www.theguardian.com/politics/2019/jun/25/brexit-boris-johnson-britain-will-leave-eu-31-october-do-or-die.

Wallace, S., Nazroo, J., & Bécares, L. (2016). Cumulative effect of racial discrimination on the mental health of ethnic minorities in the United Kingdom. *American Journal of Public Health, 106,* 1294–1300.

Walter, S. (2019). Better off without you? How the British media portrayed EU citizens in Brexit news. *International Journal of Press/Politics, 24,* 210–232.

Watson, M. (2019, May 16). *Michael Gove's war on professional historical expertise: Conservative curriculum reform, extreme whig history and the place of imperial heroes in modern multicultural Britain.* British Politics. Retrieved from https://doi.org/10.1057/s41293-019-00118-3.

Watts, J. (2016, June 29). The EU referendum has caused a mental health crisis. *The Guardian.* Retrieved from https://www.theguardian.com/commentisfree/2016/jun/29/eu-referendum-mental-health-vote.

Williams, Z. (2019, April 4). 'All I hear is anger and frustration': How Brexit is affecting our mental health. *The Guardian.* Retrieved from https://www.theguardian.com/politics/2019/apr/04/anger-and-frustration-how-brexit-is-affecting-our-mental-health.

Wood, M. J., & Gray, D. (2019). Right-wing authoritarianism as a predictor of pro-establishment conspiracy theories. *Personality and Individual Differences, 138,* 163–166.

Yamamoto, M. (1999). *Animacy and reference: A cognitive approach to corpus linguistics.* Amsterdam: John Benjamins.

YouGov. (2019a). *YouGov/5 news survey results.* YouGov. Retrieved from https://d25d2506sfb94s.cloudfront.net/cumulus_uploads/document/3vq4kkd53t/5News_BrexitMentalHealth_190118_w.pdf.

YouGov. (2019b). *YouGov/5 news survey results.* YouGov. Retrieved from https://d25d2506sfb94s.cloudfront.net/cumulus_uploads/document/9gs7ol1mhl/5News_190318_Brexit_MentalHealth.pdf.

Younge, G. (2018, February 3). Britain's imperial fantasies have given us Brexit. *The Guardian.* Retrieved from https://www.theguardian.com/commentisfree/2018/feb/03/imperial-fantasies-brexit-theresa-may.

Zmigrod, L., Rentfrow, P. J., & Robbins, T. W. (2018). Cognitive underpinnings of nationalistic ideology in the context of Brexit. *PNAS, 115,* E4532–E4540.

Index

Druck:
Customized Business Services GmbH
im Auftrag der
KNV Zeitfracht GmbH
Ein Unternehmen der Zeitfracht - Gruppe
Ferdinand-Jühlke-Str. 7
99095 Erfurt